CW00552411

ISBN (ebook): 978-1-7396222-2-0
ISBN (paperback): 978-1-7396222-3-7

Dedication

To the van life and overland community for all their help and support. You will not find a truer embodiment of the word 'community' anywhere else, and we remain in their debt for their contribution to helping us realise our dream.

Contents

Author's Notes

This is not a manual on how to convert a truck into a camper. Note the subtitle is How NOT to do it.

However, it is always useful to have someone who's already done it wrong to learn from.

This is the story of how WE converted a truck into a camper. I hope it might give you a giggle, a few ideas to show what's possible if you put your mind to it, and stop you making some of the daft mistakes we did!

A Note on Terminology

In the UK, in line with European licencing requirements, LGV (Large Goods Vehicle) has been standard terminology for the trucks formerly known as HGVs (Heavy Goods Vehicles) since 1992.

Prior to that, LGV referred to a Light Goods Vehicle, which was a van or truck with a gross weight below 3,500 kg.

Old habits die hard, though. HGV remains in common usage, and is used interchangeably with LGV to mean a Heavy, rather than a Light Goods Vehicle, which is confusing.

In this book, I use the up-to-date term LGV to refer to an HGV!

Likewise, the HGV Class 2 licence to drive rigid trucks up to 32 tonnes is now the Category C licence.

Since everyone, including the UK haulage industry, my LGV driving instructor and the LGV test centre, refers to the Class 2 licence, and everyone knows what it is, I refer to a Cat. C licence as a Class 2, just to keep things simple!

Chapter 1

Foreword

"If you'd just bought a normal, boring campervan like every sane person in the world, you wouldn't have had any of these problems. Life would be extremely dull, though."

Gwyn Moses, DipHe, BSc, BSc (Hons), MBA, BA (Hons) & BMF (Best Male Friend)

Chapter 2

Grand Designs

I have an admission to make. Property renovation programmes are my guilty pleasure – and an inspiration.

First and foremost, I'm a Hammer Head.

For years, *Homes Under the Hammer* was my weekday daytime TV paramour. 'Hammer,' as it's known to aficionados, features unsuspecting buyers purchasing property at auction. They aspire to find rubies in the rough and profit from the plain, but frequently end up with dry rot, subsidence, and a blown budget.

This happens most often when they ignore Hammer's golden rules.

1. ALWAYS view before bidding.

2. Read the legal pack.

3. Set a budget and stick to it.

I love the variety of projects they feature: from old sewage works to pieces of industrial wasteland, with every type of residential dwelling in between. But, a highlight for me is the literal soundtrack. The music is truly inspiring. They might pair the 'Before' montage of a ramshackle wreck with *This Ole House* by Shakin' Stevens. Dodgy circuitry? Cue Eddy Grant's *Electric Avenue*. My all-time favourite was the outstanding appropriation of Billy Idol's *Rebel Yell* for a many-bedroomed residence whose only toilet was outside. I'm certain that in the midnight hour, the young lady who cried for more, more, more was not lodging an impassioned request for additional indoor privies.

From the beginning, George Clarke's Amazing Spaces has been grist to the mill of my tiny home aspirations. Here, subjects create bonkers but bijou living quarters from sheds, tree houses, or an odd assortment of base vehicles such as a derelict boat, a retired London bus, or a decommissioned Sea King helicopter fuselage strapped to a flatbed truck.

But if it's wild ambition meeting unfettered eccentricity you're after, there's always the granddaddy of them all, *Grand Designs*.

Since 1999, architect Kevin McCloud, MBE, clad in a blazer with his trademark woolly scarf rippling behind in a breeze of creativity, follows the visionaries of this world. The ones who drive humanity forward with their crazy thinking, experimental ideas, and unwavering optimism. People prepared to sacrifice their sanity – along with their relationships and their grandchildren's inheritance – on the altar of their bold, unconventional, and sometimes hopelessly insane, home-building dreams.

Who can forget the "heroic" Eco Arch house, whose domed roof was a confection of ceramic tiles and plaster of Paris last seen in 14th century Spain? It partially collapsed when one of the crew leaned on it. Or the monumental challenge of Yorkshire's Hellifield Peel Tower? A stately seven-bedroom family castle raised from an 800-year-old pile of Grade-1-listed rubble, despite the central wall disintegrating and the costs exploding. Or the builds based on the shape of an ammonite fossil or a hamster wheel?

At key milestones, McCloud pops in to survey the subject's progress, proffer wise counsel, and gently allude to flaws in design and logic. Then, he presents his signature soliloquy to camera like a wandering, windblown poet.

"This collapsing beam is no mere structural support. It is the spine of Rufus' aspirations. The backbone of Camilla's dream."

When he returns to find the unfortunate couple/kids/newborns spending another unexpected winter in a caravan surrounded by freezing mud and construction chaos, McCloud may discuss the pros and cons of their approach to Project Management.

Regardless of my decades-long televisual apprenticeship, I never understood the purpose of Project Management.

Even as an absolute novice, who had disregarded Hammer's principal golden rule and bought unseen.

If you have discussed your plans with a knowledgeable contractor who is working for you, what's the point of a Project Manager? Won't the builder simply handle it for you?

And if you're a reasonably intelligent individual, capable of navigating the treacherous waters of budget overruns and construction calamities, can't you just oversee a project yourself?

Even in absentia, because coronavirus travel restrictions mean you can't return to the UK to supervise your project in person?

After all, email and international mobile telecommunications have featured on the communication landscape for decades.

I could almost see McCloud's quizzical eyebrows arch higher than the dome of the 14th century Spanish villa.

With our own Grand Design, my husband Mark and I were about to discover the merits of hands-on project management.

The hard way.

Chapter 3

Friday The 13th

On Friday 13th December 2019, our lives changed forever.

For the previous three years, Mark and I had been permanent nomads, chasing sunshine, snowflakes, and adventure.

In 2016, we had given up work, rented out our apartment, and sold most of our possessions to travel full time in Europe with our four dogs, Cavapoos (Cavalier/Poodle cross) Kai, Rosie, Ruby, and Lani.

During the summer, we sated our wanderlust in Caravan Kismet, an RV trailer towed by Big Blue, our trusty panel van and toy box.

In winter, we rented an apartment in the snow to indulge our passion for hurtling down hills with our feet strapped on to a pair of planks.

Holed up in Monte Rosa, our favourite ski resort in the Italian Alps, we heard the result of Britain's most crucial general election in a generation. As we savoured clear Alpine air and planned our next descent, the news of Prime Minister Alexander Boris de Pfeffel Johnson's electoral triumph reached us.

With his bumbling manner and mop of yellow hair, The Johnson won the hearts of the nation with promises as bold and disingenuous as his personality. He fought his campaign principally on one topic: Brexit. Britain's exit from the European Union (EU).

He pledged to 'Get Brexit Done' and claimed he had an 'Oven Ready Deal'.

Even his most stalwart supporters said it could take 50 years to sort out Brexit, but they said it very quietly, and after the election. It mattered not to them that youngsters could be collecting their pensions before they saw any Brexit benefits.

Johnson threatened Britain with an inundation of 70 million Turks, which was odd, with him being descended from a Turkish asylum seeker. Then, on the side of his Brexit bus, he promised £350 million per week for the NHS (the UK's National Health Service). I chuckled when I saw it, thinking *no one will believe that*.

But the electorate wanted to believe it.

On Friday the 13th, they returned Johnson to Downing Street with a landslide 80-seat majority.

The Brexit bombshell had detonated.

Brexit was now inevitable.

***

Johnson had already expelled all the moderate voices from his government. With fervent Brexiteers in charge – and immigration central to his Vote Leave campaign – it didn't take a genius to figure out that Johnson's version of Brexit undoubtedly signalled an end to Freedom of Movement (FOM).

FOM granted the extraordinary privilege of indefinite visa-free travel, study, work, or residence in any country within the Schengen Zone.

For British citizens, ending FOM would limit European escapades to a mere 90 days in each 180-day window throughout the entire Schengen area. Then, Schengen comprised 26 countries and counting, with Croatia, Romania, and Bulgaria committed to join.

It was the death knell for many a retirement plan, including ours. Brexit meant goodbye to the year-long jaunt around Europe in our RV. Farewell to ski seasons in the Alps, and *adios* to the prospect of sunny winters in Spain.

The implications caused me to utter a life-changing sentence to my beloved.

"I've had enough of Britain – let's go to Mongolia."

***

I've always longed to visit Mongolia.

Ever since I read about Genghis Khan and saw the film *Mongol*, I aspired to become a Mongolian horse archer, galloping across the steppes with the wind in my hair and an eagle on my wrist. Home for me would be a felt ger.

As Adventure Caravanners, Mark and I had hitched up, towed, and split our infinitives to 'Boldly Go Where No Van Has Gone Before'.

Although Big Blue and Caravan Kismet had given us problem-free conduct over the Carpathian Mountains, along the occasional footpath, and through two Romanian cornfields, Mongolia could be a step too far.

Brief research soon revealed that towing a trailer presents the greatest potential to cause issues when travelling overland on rough terrain. Mongolia is a country three times the size of France, with only three paved roads.

To negotiate the Pamir Highway and the Gobi Desert, we needed something more substantial. Casually, we started scanning the internet for a 4-wheel drive expedition vehicle.

On the very same Friday the 13th, following The Johnson's election victory, I issued my Christmas message to the nation.

"The lies to the right, 364.

"The lies have it.

"Let's hope today's decision will make you healthy, wealthy and wise – we're off to Mongolia."

Chapter 4

13th December to 13th January

When you're a complete novice, how do you specify and source an expedition truck?

The first step is to decide what you want.

Then do some research.

Lots of research!

The first Amazon delivery to our apartment in Monte Rosa was *The Overlanders' Handbook* by Chris Scott. This helped us compile a list of our requirements.

Obviously, four-wheel drive was essential.

We needed something large enough to live in full time, which could house all our sports gear, and be self-sufficient off-grid for several weeks. We established ten tonnes was the sweet spot for an overlander. Anything heavier had limitations: it might struggle to access some areas, cross certain bridges, and risked getting bogged down in soft ground.

When we started our adventures, conventional motorhomes lacked the space to transport all our windsurfers, SUPs (Stand Up Paddleboards), skis, bikes, dog trailers, and other paraphernalia. We opted for the van/caravan combo because Big Blue, a Hyundai iLoad panel van, could accommodate all our toys, and was handy for sightseeing, shopping and getting to windsurfing beaches down narrow lanes.

With no tow vehicle, we determined we'd need room for a quad bike (ATV – All-Terrain Vehicle) as a runaround, and as emergency transport in case we got stuck somewhere remote.

Mechanically, our aim was something simple, reliable, and easy to repair, with good availability of spares worldwide.

Since we intended to visit places like the Pamir Highway, along the border of Afghanistan, we didn't want to look too threatening militarily.

Our budget was flexible within reason, but not unlimited. To maintain our state of retirement, we have to watch our pennies.

Timescale – well, that was as soon as possible. Once Mark and I decide to do something, we like to get it done!

***

Once you know what you want, you must work out how to get it.

The quickest way was to buy a truck that was already converted. Hopefully, by someone with rather more knowledge about building an overlander than us...

We had toured in Caravan Kismet full time for three years, so we had a clear idea of the layout and facilities we wanted, such as a shower, loo, and the kitchen set up. I also knew I wanted a light and spacious interior.

We searched the internet. Ready-to-go options seemed relatively expensive, although when you don't fully understand the specifications of the base vehicle or the onboard equipment, it's hard to make fair comparisons. At this early stage, solar power systems were tantamount to witchcraft for me.

We liked an ex-army ambulance and a German army fire engine. On the plus side, we felt such vehicles might look sufficiently neutral to avoid being shot at. Sadly, none had anything approaching the layout we wanted, and inside, they all seemed dark and cramped.

Mark is a genius at configuring small areas to maximise space. He could visualise how to tinker with the layouts, but every off-the-shelf vehicle would need expensive remodelling to meet our requirements.

Plus, our inexperience raised another important question. Did their creators know any more about vehicle conversions than us? We had no desire to land ourselves with someone else's problem.

The second option was to build our own.

In consultation with our second Amazon delivery, Haynes' *Build Your Own Overland Camper Manual,* it looked less complicated than putting together flat-pack furniture. (Some converters *do* use flat-pack furniture for their interiors!) And we could always get help. We weren't sure from whom, but as we're fond of saying, "There's always a solution!"

Doing it ourselves had some advantages.

We would have the freedom to choose whatever layout we liked and specify high-quality fittings, such as solar panels. This would ensure we had the extended off-grid capability we needed. Plus, when things inevitably go wrong at the most inopportune moment, such as in the middle of the Gobi Desert, we'd have a fighting chance of knowing how to fix an outfit we'd built ourselves.

Since we couldn't find anything ready-made, we decided on the self-build route.

To avoid the hassle, time, and expense of mounting a cargo box ourselves, we also settled on a truck with one already fitted and ready to convert. Installing a box is not the easiest DIY (Do It Yourself) project, because there are complex technical aspects to consider. Of course, suppliers such as Zeppelin and Bespoke Bodies will design and fit one to the rig of your choice, but DIY or bespoke, either route would add months to the timescale.

We scanned military dealers and auctions all over Europe, but found very few closed-box trucks available for sale. Those with cargo boxes were 13 to 15 ft (approximately 4 to 4.5 m) long, which was smaller than our ideal. Certainly too small to fit an ATV inside.

That meant our only option to carry an ATV was on a trailer, which led straight back to the main issue: towing a trailer is the most likely source of problems on rough terrain.

In addition, we both felt an expensive ATV in plain sight was akin to having a sign stating, 'Attention. Interior packed with valuables! Please rob, then pinch me to escape!'

When a trailer capable of handling off-road terrain with a high-spec quad on board came with a hefty price tag of £8,000, we buried the trailer idea for good.

For a few weeks, we'd kept coming back to ogle a batch of magnificent bull-nosed trucks for sale from a dealer in Rotterdam. They were 6x4-wheel drive Volvo N10s. Built in 1990, the Belgian Army had just decommissioned them after 30 years' service.

They looked solid and reliable – they were Volvos, after all. Their age pre-dated complicated automobile electronics, which placed them firmly in the 'clang it with a spanner' school of vehicle maintenance. That was perfect for an expedition rig. Any mechanic should be able to fix a purely mechanical lorry.

Our Dutch friend Casper was enthusiastic when we showed him the N10s.

"My nephew drove similar trucks in Afghanistan. He said you can drive on the moon with this kind of truck!"

(I know – if the moon had enough atmosphere to support internal combustion, but you take my point!)

We checked the specification.

On paper, the Volvo N10 appeared to be a formidable expedition vehicle.

She could climb a sixty-degree slope, cross a thirty-degree incline, and forge through rivers a metre-and-a-half deep. Casper sent us a video showing a Volvo N10 doing all those things in the Amazon, with the curious addition of dancing girls in bikinis with anacondas draped around their necks.

Even without the snakes and dancing girls, we fell ever so slightly in love.

***

For the next few weeks, over mid-ski coffee in the mountain huts and crunching around in the snow under the ski lifts with our four pups, we chewed over the merits and drawbacks of such a large truck.

"She's too heavy," one would say. "24.5 tonnes gross! That's *way* over the 10-tonne sweet spot for an overland truck."

"But we won't be running her at full capacity," the other would counter. "Unladen, her tare weight is about 10 tonnes. That means we've got 14.5 tonnes of payload – as well as a 70-tonne train weight. We could tow a tank!"

"We're not getting a tank..."

"No, but we'd have no problem carrying everything we need. Realistically, converted and with enough water and fuel to be self-sufficient for at least a month, she'd only be a few tonnes over. It might mean we can't cross some bridges or reach certain places, but I'm sure mostly it will be fine. We plan to travel on rough roads, not go all-terrain rock hopping like some overlanders."

"But she's still too big. 9.6 m long and 3.85 m high." (32 ft and nearly 13 ft). "She's a beast!"

"She's actually four feet *shorter* than Big Blue and Caravan Kismet, and only a smidge wider – 2.5 m compared to 2.35m (8'2" and 7'7"). So, she could carry a quad inside."

Then Mark added, "I'm 6' 6" (2 m) tall. I need the headroom! But she's well within the 4 m legal height limit for trucks in Europe."

I knew there was a reason I'd married a transport manager. But we still had doubts.

We discussed spares. I'd discovered that Volvo spares are less widely available worldwide than those for other makes, although spares and Volvo N10's were plentiful in some countries, such as Iran.

"But when we travel," Mark said, "We're in no rush to be anywhere. So, if we have to stop and wait for parts, we'll just enjoy where we are. We can replace all the perishables, like the rubber hoses, and carry extras for obvious things, like belts and filters."

"I suppose it's similar to finding the perfect dog," I said. "The perfect expedition truck doesn't exist. It all depends on your plans and your lifestyle!"

At €26,000, her price appealed. Replacing Big Blue would cost more than that.

Of course, there was the thorny issue of fuel consumption, but unlike the public at large, who would have a lot to say about this down the line, Mark excels at lateral thinking.

"Her purchase price is an absolute steal – she costs less than a new van. We can offset her poor fuel economy against that. Not fitting a box or buying a trailer saves us thousands. Plus, we won't drive her around like a car. We'll be moving slowly from place to place, then staying for a while. On the sort of mileage we do, it will be five years before she costs us any more than running a smaller truck.

The biggest obstacle of all, though, was that we were buying her blind.

Could we really commit tens of thousands of pounds to purchase a truck we'd never seen?

"I wouldn't know what I was looking at anyway!" Mark admitted. "Brendan, at the dealer's, promised she'd come with a mechanical check. If problems arise, we will have some comeback with the dealer. But she's ex-army. She must be mechanically simple, over-engineered, and well maintained. It's a gamble, but she has a box fitted, so we won't need to pay for that – and the comparable trucks we've looked at cost several thousand pounds more."

"So, we're gambling that she won't need seven grand's worth of work," I said. "If she doesn't, we're in the money. If she does, we won't have lost. If she turns into a financial black hole, well. We'll just have to take it on the chin…"

It was important to love her.

I'd already christened her The Beast.

If she was going to be our permanent home, guardian, and accomplice on scary adventures, it needed to be love.

Mark and I met on the 9th of January. As our anniversary approached, I announced on social media,

"I might get a truck as a 21st anniversary present!"

Even so, we went round and round in circles.

However we tried to convince ourselves, we concluded she was not right for us.

Ultimately, even Mark admitted, "She's way too big and way too heavy."

We'd made our final decision.

Then the following day, we put down a deposit.

Chapter 5

13th January: Serendipity

"She may be too big and too heavy, but she'll be fun!" Mark said.

It was Monday, 13th January, the day after Mark's birthday.

"Are you sure it's not unlucky to take ownership on the 13th?"

Mark laughed.

He didn't believe in superstition.

Not yet.

***

It was exactly a month since the result of the UK's general election. In just a few weeks, on 31st January, Britain would leave the EU.

With the uncertainty that heralded for imports and exports, we needed to act quickly.

Sadly, the value of sterling had plummeted against the euro as Britain entered her new golden era of Brexit-fuelled ~~introversion~~ independence. Otherwise, our purchase would have been a much sweeter deal, but when we posted excited photos of our new truck on Facebook, serendipity happened. Our friend Miles spotted them and commented,

"Remember, I can convert that for you!"

It was a Eureka moment.

We'd bought The Beast without a fully fledged plan.

This solved our very next hurdle: 'Find an affordable way to make the metal cargo box on the back of a truck into your home.'

***

I probably don't need to do introductions, because everyone knows Miles.

En route to Romania, we stopped at a campsite in rural Hungary. The British owner knew Miles.

One evening, as we were watching a documentary on television. Miles popped up on our screen. It was no surprise.

I met Miles through a shared heritage in watersports and being Northern.

Northerners are a curiosity in the south of England, so when we find another one, we stick together.

Our tendency to call a spade a shovel (or in Miles' case, 'A bloody shovel. You idiot!') comes over a bit blunt 'down south'.

In the euphemistic regions of the Home Counties, no one ever says what they mean. Mind, when it comes to spades, they would never need to reference it directly. In affluent southern England, they call a spade, 'an implement my gardener uses'.

I am well aware of these cultural differences, because Mark and I are a mixed marriage. I'm from Lancashire. He's from Surrey.

For two decades of marriage, I have worked on his education. I am pleased to say he has now qualified for 'Born Again Northerner' status.

He supports my football team, Blackburn Rovers, tolerates mushy peas, and has agreed that the correct pronunciation of 'bath' and 'path' is as they are written, not the faux-posh *barth* and *parth*. Although he did once mock me when I saw a Lamborghini Countach sports car glide past, and uttered the word, "Class!"

"I know why you're laughing. You think my saying 'Class' not '*Clarse*' is not very *Clarssy*."

I might have called him something that rhymes with *Clarse*.

***

Over a few beers when we first met, Miles shared his story.

"Fifteen years ago, I drove to the south coast for t'day and never went back. I got a job and lived in my van for a year. I always dreamed of doing a Surfari. So, I built a bigger camper, quit the job, then drove to Morocco for a few months. Eighteen months in the end…"

Miles trained as a carpenter and metal worker, but has incredible artistic flair. Michelangelo saw David in a block of Carrera marble. Show Miles a piece of driftwood, and he would light up as his boundless creativity instantly envisioned what masterpieces he could conjure from it.

He worked from a former cow shed he called The Vision Vault. The single-storey red brick building formed one side of a delightful quadrangle of tumbledown farm buildings. Its setting was an idyllic part of rural Dorset, surrounded by woodland and fields.

As swallows darted in and out from under the eaves, and finches flitted in the hedgerows, he produced and sold his beautiful handmade creations.

He had already converted several vehicles for himself and others, and was a mine of practical knowledge gleaned through many years as a full-time van lifer. Plus, he was our mate. We thought it would be a nice idea to support a mate by giving him the business.

It had been a bad couple of years for our travels. The previous year, family illness curtailed both our summer and winter adventures. We'd returned to the UK to nurse Mark's mum and brother, who were both admitted to hospital on the same day for different reasons.

Now Brexit was a reality, we didn't want to squander our last few precious months of Freedom of Movement. We planned to remain in Italy to enjoy the rest of the ski season, then embark on a long summer trip through Poland and the Baltics.

That meant we wouldn't be around to project manage the conversion.

But we trusted Miles.

If we told him what we wanted and when, surely he could deliver.

I sent Miles a magazine article showing a truck conversion with an interior design I liked.

"I know the guy who did that."

"Of course you do," I replied.

Miles knows everyone.

"Trouble with 'im is, it'll look good for t'photos, but nowt will work."

I smiled to myself. Reassured and pleased with my choice.

"We'd like it finished by October, when we're back from our trip."

"No problem. I'll have it done by July!" Miles replied in a fit of optimism.

"There's no rush – you can just fit it around your other jobs, and work on it when you're quiet. We'll pay you as you go along."

Guaranteed income for Miles: conversion sorted for us.

It seemed like the perfect solution.

Yet, there's a saying: 'Never mix business with pleasure.'

I wonder what Mr. McCloud would have made of our project management arrangement.

Chapter 6

Squaring The Circle

So, we'd found the vehicle of our dreams, paid the deposit, specified a few extras we wanted the dealer to install before we collected her, sorted out getting the conversion done...

All that remained was to get her home to the UK.

When you buy a twenty-four-and-a-half tonne truck on a whim, there are a few technicalities to sort out.

Our particular puzzle involved importing a Belgian army vehicle, which had never been road registered, from a company based in The Netherlands, into the UK. We were in Italy – and Mark's lorry licence had lapsed the previous September because we'd convinced ourselves, "There's no point renewing it because he won't be needing *that*..."

Fools! We should have guessed that within six months, we would be the proud owners of a vintage truck.

It's fair to say we had a couple of hoops to jump through.

Thankfully for us, although the UK left the EU on 31st January 2020, it entered an eleven-month 'transition period', during which the UK's relationship with the EU did not change.

The DVLA (Driver and Vehicle Licensing Authority) confirmed that Mark could have the medical and eye tests required to renew his licence in Italy, since the UK was effectively still part of the EU, which saved him a flight home.

Of course, this first hoop was not straightforward.

My friend Ellie visited us in Monte Rosa bearing the best present. She brought two copies each of forms D2 and D4 she'd kindly picked up from a UK Post Office.

Mark took a trip to the local doctor, two villages down the mountain. *Il dottore* adhered strictly to Standard Italian Opening Hours. This meant he only appeared at the surgery on the first and third Wednesday of the month, but not after a full moon, if the fancy took him, and so long as Mercury was rising. He didn't accept appointments.

The doctor spoke no English, and Mark no Italian. Luckily, a French-Canadian patient who had married a local was in the surgery. Before you could whisper, 'patient confidentiality', he popped in to translate Mark's consultation.

Mark told me,

"Doctors are different in Italy. This one looked like a tramp. His clothes were filthy, and he had cigarette burns all down the front of his shirt!"

However, unlike when our friend and fellow seasonal nomad Caroline visited him to have a splinter removed from under her fingernail, the doctor did not sing opera to Mark to calm him.

Ellie took the completed forms home with her and posted them to the DVLA in the UK. This removed Air Mail and the capricious Italian postal system from the equation.

When Mark phoned the DVLA to check progress, they told him,

"We've returned the form to your address in England because there was a problem with the eye test."

"What was the problem?"

"We can't tell you."

Mark's brother posted the form back out to Italy and we eventually identified the problem.

In Italy, they measure eyesight out of 10. It's the decimal system, see? Back in Blighty, the DVLA will only accept the Snellen scale, measured out of 6.

We praised Ellie's foresight in bringing two copies of the forms, just in case, and took the second set on a one-hour trip down the mountain to an optician, employing the 'drive around until you find one that is open' method. The Italian optician also filled in our replacement form out of 10, but Mark used his persuasive Italian sign language and a photocopy of the Snellen scale to convince her to re-do it out of 6.

We posted it back, this time via Air Mail and the capricious Italian postal system. After a respectable interval, Mark phoned the DVLA to check progress.

"We have received the form. Everything is in order, and you can drive an LGV without the physical licence."

That was just as well, since they reported the physical licence was in the post to our English address, but it had been missing in action for a couple of weeks. At least Mark was legal to drive The Beast, but was The Beast legal to drive?

Hoop number two was insurance.

We tried all the UK's best-known high street insurance companies, who were not remotely interested. We contacted specialist companies. None would insure a vehicle with a 9.6 litre engine. Most would insure only up to 7 litres. One would cover up to 9 litres but was adamant they could not squeeze up to 9.6.

Plus, the truck was not road registered. She had no licence plates or MOT (Ministry of Transport) roadworthiness test, so she was not road legal.

Alessi, a Dutch company, offered insurance without an MOT using the chassis VIN number as identification, but they would only insure the vehicle outside your home country. This would get us to the border, but to drive in the UK, we would still need to find a UK insurer, which left us with the same problem as above.

In Britain, the law allows a vehicle with no MOT to drive directly to a testing station, so we would be fine if we could organise an MOT appointment to coincide with the truck's repatriation. Unfortunately, no test centre capable of certifying a lorry had an MOT appointment available for at least three months – but because the truck was unregistered, we couldn't get an MOT anyway.

We had yet to discover what fun registration would be.

Adrian Flux, the *maestri* of insurance for unusual or modified vehicles, said they would insure us. The bad news was that on arrival in the UK, we would have no registration plates and no MOT, so we were not road legal unless driving to a test centre – which left us with the same problem as above.

The dealer could ship The Beast to the UK on a flat-bed truck at a cost of approximately £900. This solved part of the problem, but only got The Beast to the port at Purfleet. The best quote we got for the 135-mile (217 km) onward shipping from Purfleet to The Vision Vault was approximately £1,500.

RDW, the Dutch equivalent of DVLA, was very helpful, especially when our Dutch friend Casper called on our behalf. €191.50 would secure temporary registration plates, which included two weeks' insurance. They confirmed The Beast being Belgian, not Dutch, wasn't a problem. The hitch was that they had to test the vehicle before they issued plates. Our problem was our tight timeline. We had to fit in collecting the truck in Rotterdam between a succession of guests coming out to join us in Italy. If The Beast failed RDW's test, we would simply find ourselves in the same position as before, except that precious time would have elapsed.

For €550 plus VAT (Value Added Tax), the dealer offered to source temporary Austrian plates, which included insurance for three weeks. Unless there was something we had not foreseen, that seemed to solve our problem, and was the option we plumped for in the end.

So, that would get The Beast back to England, but wasn't the end of the insurance debacle.

She needed layover insurance to cover her for fire, theft, and malicious damage while she was being converted, particularly since she would become more valuable as work progressed.

We contacted a company who specialise in flash cars. They would only cover The Beast if we kept her in a locked building. The Beast would need an aircraft hangar!

Adrian Flux quoted £380 for eight months.

No one else got back to us, so Flux got the business.

We asked Miles to clarify The Vision Vault's postcode: a conversation that would have great significance later.

"The postcode you gave us seems to relate to some residential buildings about a hundred yards along the lane. We told the insurers that it was a yard with farm buildings, not Orchard Cottage or something!"

Miles swore the postcode was correct, and the insurer seemed fine with that.

Although The Beast already had two immobilisers, the layover insurance required us to fit a Thatcham immobiliser. This seemed straightforward until we called approved Thatcham immobiliser fitters and told them our location was Bournemouth and our truck had 24-volt electrics.

"I only do 12-volt, mate. I turned up at a 24-volt once and couldn't do it."

"Yes, I am a Thatcham Approved Fitter. No, I don't fit Thatcham systems."

"Bournemouth?! Nah, mate. It's a bit too far." That was from a Thatcham fitter based in Portsmouth, fifty miles (80 km) away, who advertised a nationwide service.

At least a dozen of those we contacted didn't bother to reply. Thankfully, we eventually found a fitter in Bournemouth, who seemed confident that 24-volt was not a problem, and that six-and-a-half miles was an acceptable commute.

The next few hoops involved red tape and TMA.

The acronym for Too Many Acronyms.

We would have to complete a NOVA – a Notification of Vehicle Arrival – online within two weeks of The Beast's arrival in the UK. We would need to register her and get a log book from DVLA using the V55/5 form. It would be difficult, since she was an ex-army vehicle with no log book or registration documents. Like Paddington Bear, she would arrive in England with only a letter, albeit hers was from the Belgian army.

Then, she needed a SORN – Statutory Off Road Notification – to confirm she was not being kept or driven on public roads, otherwise she would require road tax and insurance, which we couldn't get anyway.

Since we bought The Beast in the EU while the UK was still in its post-Brexit transition period, we weren't liable for import duties or a second lot of VAT. From 1st January 2021, at the end of the transition period, importing anything from the EU would be significantly less straightforward. This still didn't stop one tax inspector from claiming we would have to pay VAT twice: in the Netherlands and in the UK.

This would not be the last time an official government body gave us incorrect information.

Next came Conformity.

This was a complex, multi-page form concerning the technical specification of the vehicle. Since The Beast was both heavier than 3.5 tonnes, and over 25-years-old, our research suggested we didn't need one, although we had a few arguments about this with the now defunct VOSA, the Vehicle and Operator Services Agency.

"You do need one!" they insisted, and incited a panic that involved calling Volvo in Gothenburg, Sweden, to see if they could provide a technical specification for a thirty-year-old model they had long since discontinued.

Although VOSA conceded in the end that we didn't need it, Volvo in Gothenburg sent a Certificate of Conformity by return. How fab is that?!

This summary can't possibly convey all the dead ends, unreturned calls, and mis-information we had to contend with.

However, we would soon know if it had all worked out – when Mark went to Rotterdam to collect The Beast at the beginning of March.

We believed we had jumped through all the hoops and got our ducks in a row, but then hoop number five materialised, and launched a totally unexpected curve ball in our direction.

A global pandemic.

Chapter 7

Carbon Footprints & The Beast

I t's time to address the elephant in the room.

Or the two-and-a-half elephants, because converted and fully laden, we estimated The Beast would weigh in at roughly 15 tonnes – the neat equivalent of two-point-five adult male African ones.

Sadly, the enthusiastic photos we shared on social media didn't just bring us Miles, they invited judgement.

"How many gallons to the mile does that do?!", "I wouldn't want your fuel bills!", or, "That's going to help global warming!" were among the more polite comments.

These remarks caught me off guard, particularly when they came from households who ran multiple cars, occupied spacious homes, and filled their spare rooms with clothes, clutter, energy-guzzling appliances, and gadgets they replaced whenever a new model appeared.

Some even owned large recreational vehicles in addition to their cars.

Don't they see the irony? I thought.

But perhaps they didn't. Because they were simply conforming to society's norm.

You may detect a tinge of defensiveness in my words, but as I mount my high horse, I invite you to join me for a gallop down the avenue of alternative thinking.

Mark and I care deeply about the environment, so such criticism felt very hurtful. We live minimally, with only those possessions we can carry. We prioritise reducing waste and have cut down our plastic consumption significantly. Plus, we never had kids. We couldn't. So, unintentionally, we've already done one of the kindest things for the planet.

There is no denying, The Beast is a huge and thirsty truck. Her fuel economy is horrible. Her specification suggested we should expect eight miles per gallon. We hoped to better that, because once converted, we predicted she'd sit ten tonnes shy of her full, laden capacity.

But breaking away from convention and embracing alternative lifestyles, such as van life, requires a shift in mindset and a departure from linear thinking.

Despite running our lifestyle on a 9.6 litre engine, I'll wager our carbon footprint is among the lowest in the UK. And should he ever read this, our detractor might suddenly find he does want to swap his fuel bills for ours. Let me explain why.

Touring overland in a caravan or motorhome is inherently more eco-friendly than most methods of living, travelling, or holidaying. Investigations by The Guardian newspaper show that a single long-haul flight can produce as much carbon dioxide as the citizens of some countries produce in a year.

The Beast won't merely be our only mode of transport: she'll be our home. And we bought a meaty 4x4 to drive the Pamir Highway, not to buzz around suburbia.

We travel in short hops, from A to B, then stay a while. Our projected mileage suggested our annual fuel costs would be comparable to a person smoking twenty cigarettes a day. Once parked up, for local errands, we have our feet, bicycles, buses, or trains.

Solar panels will generate all our electricity sustainably – and free of charge. Our two Safefill refillable LPG (Liquid Petroleum Gas) cylinders will provide all our hot water, cooking, and heating. Given that the small, well-insulated interiors of both Caravan Kismet and The Beast are similar in size, our LPG bill should remain around £200 per year, including winter in the Alps.

Aside from owning only what we can carry, repurposing The Beast prevents the waste of the resources used in her construction. While the push for Electric Vehicles (EVs) may seem environmentally friendly, it's essential to consider the broader implications. Is the generation of electricity to run them emission-free? What is the ecological impact of mining rare metals to build the batteries? And, perhaps most importantly, who stands to profit from replacing functioning diesel and LPG cars, which the government encouraged us to buy for environmental reasons, with brand new EVs?

Before passing judgement on us, I urge you to direct your environmental concerns towards the countries, governments, and industries who are the major polluters. Those who prioritise profit over environmental stewardship – not forgetting the UK's water companies. To safeguard dividends and the directors' six-figure bonuses, they discharge raw sewage into our rivers and seas because fines are cheaper than water treatment.

As for us, "Let he who is without carbon footprint cast the first stone."

By our mere existence, we all impact the environment.

If home for you is a wind-powered hovel in the Welsh hills with a turf roof and a goat for company, you are probably among the few in the Western world whose fossil-fuel consumption is lower than ours.

Drawing conclusions from isolated facts can be misleading. It's crucial to consider the whole.

The Beast is not an expensive car, she's an economical house!

Chapter 8
March 2020: Collecting The Beast

Monday: Staffal – Pont-Saint-Martin

W e fully accepted that the purchase, unseen, of an unregistered, 30-year-old Belgian army truck in Holland to import into the UK was not likely to be 100% straightforward. But with blithe determination and the conviction that 'there's always a solution', we had jumped through the many administrative hoops and squared that circle.

Yet throughout the build-up to Mark going to pick her up, it seemed the gods were trying to tell us something.

C-Day I, the first Collection Date, came and went.

Constantly on tour in darkest Africa, Brendan, the Head Honcho of the dealership, Jacaranda, was impossible to contact. Repeated efforts to get The Beast's chassis VIN number failed. This not only stalled our many and varied attempts to arrange insurance, it also left the dealer's engineer in the dark over which truck needed the back-up fuel tank we had purchased fitted. With less than a week to C-Day I, with no VIN, no insurance, and no time to fit a fuel tank, Mark made an executive decision and cancelled his carefully planned trip.

As C-Day II: The Sequel approached, Mark re-booked all the trains and buses required to convey him from high in the Italian Alps, across France, to Rotterdam in the Netherlands.

There were flights from Turin to Rotterdam, but going overland had a romantic appeal, and was more eco-friendly than a flight. This decision would quickly become a source of deep regret. But as with buying a truck on impulse, it seemed like a good idea at the time.

A few days prior to his departure, Mark accidentally grasped a baking tray fresh from the oven and seared his right hand. That night, he had to sleep with his hand in a bowl of iced water, the pain was so severe.

In the news, a story was breaking. It concerned some mystery virus from China. There was little detail other than parts of Northern Italy seemed to be affected, although they were miles from our winter hide-out in Monte Rosa. Nobody paid it much attention.

The Thursday before C-Day II, I contracted a sniffly cold. With hindsight, the symptoms did not resemble those of COVID-19-that-no-one-had-really-heard-of-yet and I was better within three days. My main concern was whether Mark would get sick. The timing looked ripe for him to be feeling poorly by the following Tuesday, when, with a raw and blistered right hand, he would need to take charge of a 24.5 tonne juggernaut for the first time in years.

For the initial part of the journey, I had planned to drive Mark to catch his first train from Pont-Saint-Martin, an hour down the mountain from our home village of Staffal. The forecast suggested the weather would be clear in the morning, but predicted heavy snow in the afternoon.

At 7:00 a.m., we opened our shutters to a blizzard.

While I am familiar with the theory of snow chains and have watched Mark put them on many times, I have never used them in anger myself. It was pointless for me to risk getting stranded in a snowstorm on my way back up to Staffal with The Pawsome Foursome, so Mark said he'd catch the bus down to Pont-Saint-Martin.

At the last moment, he decided not to carry our powder skis home to put in storage. Secretly, I welcomed his decision, especially when I felt the weight of his other two bags. Straining his back would be an unwelcome addition to our seemingly never-ending list of problems to overcome.

My exhaustive internet search yielded no trace of a local bus timetable. Our final solution was for Mark to walk down to the bus stop to check the times. While he did his Scott of the Antarctic thing, I eventually discovered a timetable online, which roughly concurred with the information he brought back.

So, at 10:15 a.m., Mark left for the bus that we believed was at 10:40, but might have been at 10:30. I was in tears and Mark's special little fur-buddy, Kai, was beside himself with grief. He knew!

Just half an hour later, at 10:45 a.m., Mark called,

"You know the narrow bit on the SR44 mountain road? The bus is having a stand-off with a 4×4! We've been stuck for a full ten minutes of raised voices and proper Italian gesticulation. The bus won't reverse on principle and the 4×4 won't – or more likely – can't."

Then, we had telephone silence thrust upon us while things went rapidly downhill.

Pont-Saint-Martin – Ivrea – Turin – Paris

Mid-afternoon, I received a garbled call from a mystery number,

"I can't stay on long. I've no signal, so I'm ringing from a Greek man's phone. They've delayed my train. I'll miss my connection in Paris."

Much later, when communication was restored, Mark filled me in regarding the bus stand-off.

The queue piled up and the 4×4 driver refused to move. The bus had to reverse up a difficult, winding road between tall buildings!

Well done, Mr. 4×4!

At least that delay gave me a few extra minutes of warmth before sitting at Pont-Saint-Martin's railway station for an hour in the rain. The single stop to Ivrea should have been simple. I hopped on when it finally arrived, but nothing happened. After fifteen minutes, everyone jumped off, and we had to run across the platform to board another train.

I reached Turin with ninety minutes to kill before a connection to Paris, so I went for a coffee and cake. Even that was anything but simple! Torino Porta Susa station is massive*, but it had no cafés or bars. I got directions, and bought a sandwich somewhere in the maze of side streets outside.*

Back at Porta Susa, thirty minutes before the Paris train was due to leave, I scanned the departures board, but there were no clues. Eventually, a platform came up, showing a 30-minute delay. I plonked next to a French African chap who spoke no English. We communicated in sign language as the delay grew to 60-minutes, then 80, 90, 110 and finally, 135.

By now, I was cold and miserable once again – and knew my Paris connection was a lost cause. On top of that, I had no phone signal. That's

where the nice Greek chap came in. He lived and worked between Paris and Turin, and loaned me his phone to call.

Ευχαριστώ – Efcharistó. Thanks, you wonderful stranger!

Late in the afternoon, our friend and fellow seasonal nomad, Graham, kindly rang me to ensure I wasn't marooned somewhere on a snowy hairpin. Graham and his wife Caroline were staying two villages down the valley. Originally, they had offered to drop Mark off at the station in Pont, where they had planned a pre-snow supermarket sweep.

We declined, because by driving Mark down, I would gain an extra hour with my beloved.

In view of the raging blizzard, they too had wisely aborted their drive to Pont. They understood perfectly well why Mark had opted for public transport.

That evening, my best friend called to tell me that, because of peer pressure, she couldn't see Mark while he was in the UK. She had kindly accepted the delivery of a new pair of skis for me.

"I'll leave them outside for Mark and wave at him through the window. I can't go out to say, 'Hi'. My cycle club said they'd refuse to see me if we had any contact."

Things were quite calm in Italy, but the UK media circus had begun.

Emotive stories of a Chinese zombie, flesh-eating virus were beginning to whip the British public into a hysteria of panic buying. My Facebook feed filled with pictures of empty supermarket shelves and unfathomable reports of people stock piling toilet rolls.

Coming from Northern Italy made Mark Public Enemy Number 1.

"We're up a mountain at 1,800 m, and a whole county-and-a-half away from the virus outbreak in Lombardy," I said. "We're in the Aosta Valley. It's 1,200 square miles and has zero cases of COVID-19."

I completely understood my friend had been placed in an impossible situation, but I felt upset, alone, and abandoned.

I sought solace in a bracing nip of single malt.

Tuesday: Paris – Brussels – Rotterdam

Six minutes past midnight – I got a call from Paris.

It was lovely to hear Mark's voice.

"I've finally arrived at *Gare de Lyon*!"

This is my favourite Parisian station, because I enjoy thinking it's named after Richard I. (It always pleases me to refer to the *Coeur de Lion* as *Gare de Lyon*!)

He'd missed his train, so my hasty internet search confirmed that his best hope of making the C-Day II rendezvous in Rotterdam was a coach from Paris via Brussels. This involved a nocturnal Parisian city crossing to the bus station, so I immediately launched into a frenzy of dread that a knife-wielding robber might attack him. I pleaded with him to take a taxi, but he said he'd quite enjoy the walk.

"I'll catch up with lost sleep on the overnight journey to Brussels," he assured me, so I kept to myself the secondary worry about him taking command of a 24.5 tonne truck while sleep-deprived and with an injured hand, after a two-day transportation ordeal.

The following morning, Caroline rang to check on me.

"I haven't heard from Mark," I said. "I'm so worried about him crossing Paris last night."

In her best headmistress voice, Caroline demanded, "How tall is Mark?"

"Six-foot-six."

"Exactly. It would be a brave robber…"

Caroline's no-nonsense approach snapped me out of my catastrophizing. I felt better for a while, at least.

Later, Mark rang from Brussels. Although he had listened to me and took a half-hour taxi ride across Paris from *Coeur de Lion*, he rather wished he hadn't.

I arrived to find a bus stop.

No café.

No seats.

No shelter.

No nothing.

With my departure at 2:30 a.m., I killed the intervening two hours by wandering the streets in the freezing cold.

It makes you really empathise with the homeless. Just the sense of having nowhere to go is awful, but being stuck outdoors in this, even for a few hours, is brutal.

A small crowd joined me: a young Argentinian couple heading for their next adventure after living in Denmark for a year: a nice girl from Cameroon: a duo from Lille, which is a stop en route to Brussels, and another bonus Argentinian. Ten minutes late, at 2:40 a.m., the coach arrived. It was packed, so I had a very uncomfortable, six-hour, red-eye crossing of France into Belgium.

My next update came around breakfast time, from aboard the bus from Brussels to Rotterdam.

The bus was delayed, but at least it has phone-charging facilities – and the company is familiar. I sat with the same chap I was with on the coach from Paris! He's 25 and is from Italy, but he works in Brussels. He wants to study for a degree in agriculture.

I hope I didn't bore him grumbling about Brexit and the lack of kindness in the world. Mind, he complained about the racism in Italy, so it's not a trait unique to Little Britain. His mum's from Martinique and his dad from Burkina Faso.

I emailed the dealer, Jacaranda, to say Mark would arrive with them around 1 p.m.

My primary off-the-scale worry was that our 30-year-old Beast might not start, never mind be roadworthy.

I bailed out of spending the morning skiing with Graham. I'd had a dreadful night, and not solely because of worrying about Mark.

When I took the pups out for their final pee poo in the gardens that surrounded the apartment, a blood-curdling screech shattered the snowy stillness.

A hysterical Kai, our cuddly black-and-white boy, bolted out of the darkness straight towards me, shrieking and shaking.

I swept him up and checked him over. He didn't seem to be injured. I stroked him to calm him, then left him safe inside the foyer, while I raced back outdoors to gather the three girls.

They showed their support to Kai by starting up a symphony of barking. I was mortified; it was 10:30 p.m. A bit too late to treat all my neighbours in the apartment block to a Cavapoo cacophony.

But while I was outside, I heard Kai screeching again.

It echoed all around the tiled foyer. I rushed indoors to find absolutely no sign of him. It was my turn to become hysterical.

As panic erupted inside me, I started screaming,

"Where's my dog? WHERE'S MY DOG?! WHAT HAVE YOU DONE WITH MY DOG?"

I thought I had heard voices and that some unsympathetic fellow resident had taken him as a punishment. Either for the racket, or the *cacca*.

Every dog in the village roamed free: a policy with obvious consequences.

Even though we were the only people who ever picked up poo – often, piles of *cacca* unconnected to The Fab Four – everyone directed abuse regarding dog poo towards us. Or, should I say, towards me, since, as Caroline pointed out, Mark is six-foot-six, and it's always easier to pick on the woman.

Somehow, Kai had squeezed past a heavy metal door and into the stairwell, where he was caterwauling more loudly than a battle of the bands between Motörhead and Deep Purple. He was clearly terrified, but there was no-one else in sight. I picked him up and cuddled him. Once again, I could feel his little body trembling uncontrollably. With Kai in my arms, I collected the other dogs and, like a canine Pied Piper, led everyone inside towards the sanctuary of our apartment.

A tired and worried-looking Luisa, the building's housekeeper, was waiting for me at the top of the stairs.

"I'm so sorry about the noise," I said in halting Italian.

Even though she would be the one forced to field complaints about the commotion, Luisa said it was no problem

Luisa adored the pups. The Pawsome Foursome and her little dog, Lampo ('Lightning') were best buddies. Most days, I had to reduce The Fab Four's dinners because, every time she saw them, Luisa plied them with entire boxes of doggie treats.

Luisa's only concern was Kai. "What's the matter with him?" she asked.

I told her, "*Non so. Ha paura del buio?* – I don't know. Perhaps he's afraid of the dark?"

I had absolutely no idea what had terrified Kai to that degree.

Recently, I'd learned about Monte Rosa's resident wolf population.

Der Schopf – 'The Office' was a favourite mountain refuge on the glorious 8 km (5 mile) Olen ski run down to Alagna. We called it Pepé's after one incumbent – a gorgeous, white-and-grey dappled English Setter. On our last visit, his owner, Stefano, told us he'd moved Pepé into town, "because of the wolves."

But lupine stalking seemed unlikely on the outskirts of a busy ski village.

Certainly, there were foxes around who made lavish contributions to the poo problem. Ironically, one of the *cacca* complainants put out food for them! But foxes are shy and solitary. I couldn't imagine a lone *volpe* taking on a cavalcade of baying Cavapoos.

Overall, it was not a very relaxing evening.

Once again, whisky was called for.

That helped me relax, but with the pack disrupted, the pups were restless and behaving oddly. Mystifyingly, our little black fluff ball, Lani, started patrolling the periphery of the apartment while running her tongue along the floor, in the manner of a bonkers upside-down dodgem car. During the night, Rosie woke me an unprecedented three times to go outside. Perhaps she wondered if Mark was there.

Kai would never willingly go out in the dark again.

***

At 12:30 p.m. on Tuesday, I got the call.

Finally, Mark was in Rotterdam!

It had taken twenty-six hours – and no matter how short, no single leg of the journey had gone to plan.

So much for the romance of overland travel and letting the train take the strain!

Lady Luck had made it clear she was not on our side.

After the traumas we'd endured just purchasing The Beast and getting Mark as far as Rotterdam to collect her, I was still riddled with angst.

Was The Beast mechanically unimpaired? Would she even start? Had the temporary Austrian plates that included insurance been delivered?

And would Mark, who had not sat behind the wheel of a truck for years, remember how to drive one?

Tuesday: Rotterdam – Calais (By Accident)

My last update from Rotterdam had been about midday, before Mark and The Beast had actually met.

It was 9:00 p.m. that evening before I got a call to say,

"I'm about eighty miles from the Channel Tunnel," which was a shame.

I had just paid a £48 supplement for the ferry crossing he had booked from Le Havre.

Our Brittany Ferries Club Voyage discount card is in my name. They emailed to inform me that, because I was at home puppy-sitting and not travelling alongside Mark, an additional fee applied. In order to support Mark as best I could with his horrendous journey, I paid straight away. After all, it was one less thing to worry him.

Unfortunately, my action added the anxiety of whether we could get a refund for the surcharge, as well as the original fare, which he now no longer needed.

I'd been a great help!

Mark couldn't chat because once again, his phone battery was almost flat, but I deduced from his location that the truck had started and he had made such good time that he wanted to get an early crossing on Eurotunnel.

My interpretation was about as far from the truth as I could get, so I will pass you over to Mark for the first-hand account.

***

I grinned from ear to ear when I first heard the throaty roar of The Beast. She is a very beautiful truck. The dealer gave me a brief driving lesson around the block. It was tough, and I was absolutely rubbish, which was disheartening. I am accustomed to driving a large vehicle; the van and caravan are the length of an articulated lorry, but it's a while since I drove a truck. Eight gears (plus reverse!) takes a bit of getting used to, but it would soon come back... I hoped.

I said my goodbyes to the kind folk at Jacaranda, who had been so helpful. I jumped into the cab to start my journey, but all was not well. Although fully charged when I left home, the satnav was dead. I had no road map for the Netherlands or Belgium and, after all the delays, it was approaching the evening rush hour. The weather didn't look great, and the previous night, I only had two hours' sleep. The Beast has 24-volt electrics, which immediately thwarted any possibility of charging the phone, or more importantly, the satnav. Jax asked me to take loads of photos, as she couldn't be with me for the first meeting with The Beast, but even the camera wouldn't work.

I had made a list of interim destinations to help me navigate, but as I left Rotterdam, there were no signs for any of the way points. When I started to doubt if I was heading in the right direction, I pulled off the main road to compose myself and decide whether to carry on blindly.

It was a terrible idea.

I found myself on a single-track lane, barely wider than The Beast. It was a causeway, bordered by two slender ribbons of grass, then two of Holland's famous canals: one on each side. I had no choice but to continue. After eight hundred yards, I ended up in what appeared to be a leisure centre car park. Even better, it was packed with cars and surrounded by a moat. The Beast's turning circle makes HMS Ark Royal look agile, so I performed a multi-point manoeuvre and followed my only option – back whence I came. Naturally, I met a car coming the other way. Somehow, I eased on to a slightly broader piece of the grassy border without plunging into the canal, which gave him just enough room to squeeze past.

Out of ideas, I carried on towards the centre of Rotterdam. Within thirty minutes, I picked up signs to Breda. Then, in the heaviest hailstorm I have ever experienced and the height of the rush hour, I drove an unfamiliar truck through the cities of Antwerp, Ghent, and finally crossed into France at Lille.

I can summarise the journey as follows;

TRAFFIC – TRAFFIC – TRAFFIC – HAILSTONES – DOWN-POUR – TRAFFIC – LOST!

It was a baptism of fire. At Lille, I ended up in the pitch dark on the road to the Channel Tunnel rather than the ferry at Le Havre, so I thought, Bugger it! *and continued.*

I stopped to hop online and book a ticket. I got right through to payment –then the phone battery died. My last working piece of technology. Aaaarrrrgggghhhh! I carried on regardless and reached The Tunnel around midnight. I went to the 'Passenger' check-in, because I was not 'Freight'.

"You're too big to go in 'ere, mate," the bloke said. "You'll have to go to Freight."

"Will it cost me any extra?"

"Nah, mate. It's still the same price; £130."

"I LOVE the lorry!" he shouted after me as The Beast and I executed another spectacular, multi-point U-turn, this time through an obstacle course of bollards designed to accommodate cars. It was like a dressage test for trucks. The exit spewed me out straight on to the motorway, heading away from the Tunnel. Oh sh**! *I thought. In the dead of night, I negotiated several roundabouts and eventually found the route back to the Freight Terminal.*

As part of my trip planning about a month ago, I had called Eurotunnel to check prices. I had given them The Beast's full dimensions and details. They also quoted £130 and assured me she could travel as a motorhome. But at Freight, the charge more than doubled.

"That's £280."

I explained my call to Bookings and relayed my conversation from only thirty minutes earlier.

"It's easy to say that!" Mr. Belligerent replied. He must have been very disappointed when he called the chap at the passenger gate, who confirmed he had indeed stated that the price was £130 and wouldn't change.

"It's still £280," came his obstinate response.

Clearly, this wonderful human being had not contacted his colleague with any intention of clarifying or re-evaluating his decision. His sole objective was to embarrass me and call me out as a liar.

"Surely there is someone who can give me the quoted price out of goodwill? I phoned ahead to check and have driven all the way here based on the information I was given, and with the fuel economy of this truck, that wasn't cheap..."

His answer was succinct, direct, and to the point.

"No."

The intransigent response and flexible approach to pricing reflected the same sentiment of goodwill and outstanding customer service that we have experienced previously from Eurotunnel. I recalled the occasion when they hiked up the cost to change a booking from £2 to £88 overnight. A mere 4,500%, which they assured us was justified because they had told me, "If you wait, the price might go up a bit." I wonder how much of a rise they would consider 'a lot'.

Fed up – I left them to it. After wasting a couple of hours, my resolve to boycott Eurotunnel was redoubled.

Rather like their prices.

***

Back en route to Le Havre, I pulled over at 3:00 a.m. for a sleep in the cab. About two hours later, I woke up frozen, so I drove on.

I stopped plenty of times for caffeine, chocolate, and croissants to keep me awake, and reached the port at 9:00 a.m. Wiser, after the Channel Tunnel experience, I headed to the Freight check-in, which was open. You guessed – on the ferry it was the opposite way round. By now, reversing was almost second nature. Like a pro, I backed out my near ten-metre pantechnicon and parked up because the passenger check-in was closed until 3:00 p.m.

I sat for a few hours, then immobilised The Beast. The weather was pleasant, so I went for a walk. At the far end of town, the wind and rain started.

Wet. Cold. Tired and miserable. I needed something to punch!

Wednesday: Le Havre – Bournemouth

Once again, I hadn't had a peaceful night myself. Since Mark left, Rosie cried to go out several times each night. The Fab Four's nocturnal requests are rare, and almost always genuine, so to disregard their pleas is a game of Russian roulette with canine bodily functions. I suspected she was stringing me along, but ignoring Rosie was not an option anyhow. She simply cried until I let her out.

Bleary-eyed in my pyjamas, I stood outside in the snow at 3:45, 4:45 and 5:15 a.m., carrying Lani, who would bark and wake up the whole village if I left her behind.

Then Mark called at 7:30 a.m. It surprised me to learn he was fifty miles short of Le Havre, until he explained how, true to form, The Chunnel had once again let us down spectacularly. Silently, I thanked the travel gods that I hadn't been super helpful and cancelled his ferry booking and supplement because I believed he was speeding towards Blighty via Eurotunnel.

He was brimming with excitement about our new purchase.

"I put €250 of fuel in The Beast and the gauge is still in the red! But that's not the most unbelievable thing. How many miles do you think she has on the clock?"

A 30-year-old, ex-army truck. I considered for a moment.

"4,683 km. That's all!" he interrupted. "I asked the dealer if it was genuine and they said it was, but it has to be. She has plastic sheets covering her seats, like a new truck!

Her date of manufacture – 1990 – yielded a clue.

It's not unusual for companies or the military to place orders for capital purchases years in advance.

But in 1989, the world changed.

The Berlin Wall came down, and all over eastern Europe, communist governments fell. Then, in 1991, the Soviet Union broke up and the Cold War ended. For the first time since the end of World War II, the tense stalemate between the USA and Russia eased.

Presumably, this rendered our truck surplus to requirements, so they placed her in strategic storage. Except for regular trips to the maintenance yard, it seemed she had stayed there until, after thirty years, she was decommissioned.

Some time later, Mark phoned from Le Havre.

"All the customs men have come out to gape at her. She gets more attention than The Fab Four! She's very beautiful, but she is MASSIVE," he said. "I know we knew that when we bought her, but you don't realise how big she is until you stand next to her!"

As we chatted, he shared that lunch had been a less than successful affair.

Mark and I are not fussy eaters. We are constantly adventurous with food, despite how rarely this turns out to be a winning strategy. Replete with rancid yak's butter and greasy, salted tea, The Tibetan Breakfast I endured in Nepal remains an outstanding example of this. Especially when the alternative was a full English fry up, complete with British bacon!

There are very few things that we don't eat, but when pushed to admit our dislikes, our reply is always, "Spam and whelks."

My own aversion to both ingredients in this strange iteration of surf 'n' turf originated at school. Pork luncheon meat in various forms was a persistent, puce presence in school dinners. I christened it 'Pink Plasticine', since likening it to modelling clay provided a well-founded summation of all its major attributes: appearance, smell, texture, and taste. Served cold with salad, it was unappetising, but sautéed with chips, or worse, deep-fried in batter, it oozed with grease and packed such a Plasticine punch that, forty-odd years later, the mere thought of it makes me feel queasy.

Whelks are an entirely different matter. I dissected one in a biology class. Whelk physiology has appropriated most of the creature's body surface to form a hypobranchial mucous gland. Once twisted out of its shell, the seemingly boundless curtains of mucus that oozed and drooled from the naked mollusc both fascinated and repulsed me. Remarkably, in spite of post-dissection foresight, I did try to eat one once. A vulcanised rubber eraser would have had a softer texture and, undoubtedly, more flavour.

Most people overcook fish and seafood, which dries it out and makes things like squid rubbery. However, I am not sure that any form of scald, scorch, or simmer could soften the gristly pseudopodium of a Whelk.

Anyhow, that is the background. Here's Mark to give you the full synopsis of lunch.

I found a café to warm up and grab a bite to eat. Thankfully, they let me charge the phone at reception. I have forgotten most of my French, so I ordered Fruits de Mer. I got rubber in shells (whelks); phlegm on a shell (oysters) and some prawns. The prawns were okay, even though Jax's favourite fact to share over a seafood dinner is, "Prawns are related to woodlice!" I did better with a main course of skate wing, followed by pear tart for dessert. Then coffee. Lots more coffee.

The whelks got their revenge, however. Mark finished our post-prandial conversation with a rather urgent,

"I've gotta go to the loo. NOW!"

That morning, I had skied with Graham. When we stopped for coffee in the sunshine at Pepé's/*Der Schopf,* Stefano told us the town of Alagna was half empty. Concern about this coronavirus thing was beginning to spread.

I was tired after half a day on skis, then an afternoon walk with the pups.

I did not imagine how soon or how much I would miss having a pleasantly exhausting day outdoors.

Thursday 5th March: The Vision Vault

At 1:00 a.m., Mark called.

"I'm in a bed and breakfast in Bournemouth, but I'll have to get up early to move The Beast. It was tricky to find somewhere to park such a huge vehicle. She's partly blocking a drive, but it looks disused. I simply couldn't face another night sleeping in the truck."

At 8:00 a.m., Mark rang from The Vision Vault, Miles' creative space.

Finally, The Beast had arrived.

Her transformation could begin.

Although no one could have predicted what happened next.

Coronavirus

While back in the UK, Mark had set aside a week to brief Miles on the conversion and resolve a few problems on the home front.

We'd had a fire in one of our rental apartments, so it was an opportunity to co-ordinate the repairs, sort out the insurance claim, get our tenants re-settled (they had to be moved to emergency accommodation), and restore our income as soon as possible.

It was early March 2020, and as I mentioned, there was some low-key news coverage that a mystery virus from China had landed in Italy.

We remembered the frenzies around Bird Flu, Swine Flu and SARS, which the press assured us were all going to kill us in our beds, so we weren't taking it terribly seriously. Our region of northern Italy was unaffected by the virus anyway. Nevertheless, as a responsible adult, Mark followed the emerging guidelines and avoided indoor contact with anyone.

Our closest friend refused to see him anyway, but Mark cancelled all face-to-face appointments, ate his breakfast in his room, and managed all the issues remotely. Casper and Monique, our Dutch friends, had visited us in Italy the previous week. When they got back, they said friends and neighbours in their village crossed the street to avoid them.

Then, on Sunday 8th March 2020, alone in our residence in northern Italy, I awoke to the headline:

'Coronavirus: Northern Italy quarantines sixteen million people.'

Italy reported the largest number of confirmed coronavirus cases outside China.

With hospitals filling with COVID-19 patients, the Italian PM, Giuseppe Conte, took unprecedented action. He locked down one quarter of his country's population, issuing 'stay at home' orders to stop the virus spreading.

On the evening of that same day, March 8th, he extended the measures to close public spaces, such as museums – and all the ski resorts in the Val d'Aosta – with immediate effect. That included our resort, Monte Rosa.

Suddenly, I was alone in an apartment with four dogs, in the centre of Europe's first coronavirus hotspot.

That morning, I received a concerned call from Caroline and Graham, two villages down the mountain in Gressoney St. Jean.

"We've decided to leave immediately, in case they extend the lockdown restrictions to Piedmont and the Aosta valley."

Perhaps with the tramp-like singing doctor in mind, Caroline said,

"I want to be somewhere where I understand the healthcare system and the language... Do you want to come with us?"

"Thanks," I said, "but there's no way I can single-handedly pack up the apartment and caravan in a few hours. I'll be better off waiting for Mark."

"I feel terrible leaving you with Mark away."

"I'll be fine," I assured her. "I spent weeks up the mountain on my own in a blizzard last year, when Mark first flew home to care for his mum and brother."

"Our neighbours think we're overreacting..."

"I think you're doing the right thing," I said. "I think we've all underestimated this virus..."

Mark frequently mocks me for over-worrying, so when I called him, I crossed everything, hoping he wouldn't dismiss my pleas.

"You'd better come back to Italy straight away. Milan has locked down and they've closed the ski resort today. *Pleeeease* get a flight... not the train. There's a risk of borders closing, so you really don't want to be stuck on a bus replacement service."

Within the hour, Mark rang to say,

"I've booked a flight from Gatwick to Turin at 6:40 a.m. tomorrow. I can take the train from the airport to Pont-Saint-Martin, which will save you a two-hour drive to *Torino*."

I closed my eyes and felt the relief fill my body. For once, he not only listened, but also took me seriously.

When I collected him from the station at Pont at midday the following day, Monday, Mark told me,

"I was on a 200-seater plane with eighteen passengers. Everyone had an emergency exit seat. It explains why there was no charge for extra legroom."

In the world's list of desirable destinations, China and Italy had plummeted off a cliff.

As we drove back up the hairpins to Staffal, we agreed that after four months in Monte Rosa, we both had severely itchy feet. We pledged to pack up and leave with the caravan on Thursday 12th to begin our tour of Poland and the Baltics. This shows how seriously we'd underestimated coronavirus.

With the way our luck was running, we had no intention of departing on another Friday 13th. But what a difference a day makes.

On Tuesday morning, 10th March 2020, the headline changed. Fortuitously re-united, Mark and I could read it together over a coffee.

'Coronavirus: Italy extends emergency measures nationwide. The measures will remain in place until 3rd April 2020.'

We had planned to leave, but our time had run out.

Italy was closed.

We were trapped.

But by virtue of one day, our little family was able to sit it out together.

Not everyone was so lucky.

***

I adapted parts of this chapter from my book It Never Rains But It Paws, *which follows how our Exit Before Brexit, to avoid the possibility of being trapped in Britain in the event of a No Deal Brexit, turned into four months of strict isolation in Italy.*

When Italy's lockdown ended, the UK border was still closed, which left us unable to return home. Instead, we went on a road trip around Poland, which I document in To Hel In A Hound Cart: A Journey to the Centre of Europe.

Chapter 9

Our Own Grand Design

We had a truck twin.

Mike saw our pictures of The Beast online and expressed an interest in a blue Volvo N10 that the dealer had for sale. He wanted to know how we'd imported The Beast.

Along with several of our friends, Mike was keen to see our proposed interior layout for The Beast.

"Do you have CAD drawings of it?" he asked.

"Computer Aided Design? Um, Mark has been tinkering around with an Excel spreadsheet. Does that count?"

I felt it should.

After all, a spreadsheet was design, aided by a computer. I sent what I had through to Mike, in case it would help. I'm not sure our plans impressed him!

The Romans built an empire with lines in the sand and scribbles on wax tablets. Leonardo da Vinci designed the world's first helicopter with a quill. As a kid, I used to mess about with felt-tipped pens and graph paper. Colouring in cells to create a scale drawing on an Excel spreadsheet seemed a tremendous step up from any of that.

Mark had Top Views, Side Views and everything, which was a good job. His hasty exit from the UK cut short his discussions with Miles regarding the truck's interior.

In his parting email, Mark said,

Shame I had to rush away early, but I can't afford to get locked out of Italy. I have attached a one-page Excel spreadsheet summary of the layout we discussed, but I'll leave the 'look' in your capable hands.

In a vast underestimation of the impact of the coronavirus pandemic, I added,

I missed my Mr. I'm glad I'm getting him back. Sorry he hasn't had time to sort everything out with you properly, but we trust your judgement. Perhaps Mark can visit again in a month or two when this has all calmed down.

Due to border closures and travel restrictions, it would be almost six months before we could legally enter the UK once again.

Mark and I loved Miles's taste and artistic flair, so we were happy to entrust the finer details to him. We set up a bank account for him and deposited a float, so that he could purchase materials as and when he needed them, without having to ask us each time.

Since he was a mate, we wanted him to benefit from the project as much as possible. Based on the well-known saying, 'Buy a man a piece of bent metal and he has bent metal for a day. Buy a man a metal bender and he has bent metal for life,' we bought Miles the metal bending machine he coveted.

It would save us money on components, and leave him the legacy of a useful tool.

Delighted, Miles replied,

"This will be a breeze. You two are so relaxed about it, it makes it easier for me to flow. I understand what you want and need, and I have free rein to achieve it."

In the end, our truck twin didn't buy the N10, which we had christened 'Even Bigger Blue'. (We would have bought her had she not been around £7,000 more expensive than The Beast, who retained her original NATO green livery.)

He acquired a different truck and appointed a professional converter to execute the transformation. Many months later, he posted footage of his entire CAD-designed, pre-assembled interior being placed inside his custom-made box to check it fitted, then taken out again to add the finishing touches.

Our build couldn't have been more different.

Already, at this early stage, we had committed ourselves firmly to the 'winging it' approach.

***

The first major change to the design came quickly, when we abandoned the idea of carrying an ATV/quad bike inside.

The truck's floor was more than a metre above the ground. As Miles pointed out, "You'll need ramps about a mile long to get a quad in that! You won't use it, because it'll be a faff getting it in and out. Besides, it will be really dangerous. Quads are heavy. You don't want to risk breaking a bone or being crushed if it falls off the ramps, especially in the middle of nowhere."

An electric lift would be safer, but that was simply something else to go wrong.

On the upside, without the quad, our interior space had just increased by the size of a small family car. It would be HUGE. The Beast truly was going to be the manor house of motorhomes.

Mark altered his computer aided design.

"You need a table and an oven," Miles insisted.

"We had both in the caravan," we countered. "We never used either. A table gets in the way and we'd prefer an extra cupboard to an oven."

When you live in a small space, storage is key!

The second casualty was the 'cab tunnel' or 'crawl-through'.

We had wanted direct access from the living quarters into the cab. A security feature which would enable us to drive away from a dodgy situation with no need to exit the vehicle. Even better, if we got stuck in traffic, I could nip into the back and make a cup of tea. And, if we parked in a sea of mud in a howling gale – something that happened more times than we care to mention in Caravan Kismet – we could enter our home without getting drenched, accompanied by sixteen clean, dry paws.

The issue with the crawl-through was the significant distance between the cab and cargo box on the Volvo N10. They move independently of each other, which would make it quite a feat of engineering to connect them securely with a tunnel. The spare wheel occupied the offside of the gap, so the access would have had to be on the near side: directly behind the driver's seat. Impracticalities aside, a crawl-through would occupy a whole wall. Put another way, it would take fifteen per cent of our vertical space out of use for storage.

While nice to have, we had to weigh the complexities of installation against the likelihood of an emergency that made it necessary. We decided it was a risk we would have to live with.

We left Miles to get on with the conversion, not realising the impact coronavirus would have on us all. Miles's free rein already had his imagination running riot.

"How do you feel about being able to put up hammocks inside?"

***

But to introduce you to the proposals for our Grand Design with the aplomb they deserve, I must hand you over to virtual Kevin McCloud to escort you on his customary initial tour.

As we look at the plans for The Beast, Jackie and Mark's ambitious overland truck conversion, we're immediately struck by the sheer ingenuity and practicality that defines this mobile sanctuary, where every inch serves a purpose.

In the realm of compact living, storage reigns supreme and organisation is the key to harmony. Here, it's elevated to an art form.

Starting at the rear, a larger-than-super-king-size bed commands attention. First and foremost, it's a cocoon of comfort where they can retreat from nomadic uncertainty. Yet, its expansive surface conceals a cavernous garage area ready to accommodate a veritable arsenal of adventure accessories, from windsurfers to electric bikes, and vital off-road recovery gear.

The massive back doors not only grant access to the garage, but bring the outside in. Fling them open and they don't just offer a glimpse of the great outdoors, but throw you an invitation to embrace it. From your own divan, the boundaries of indoor comfort and outdoor exploration blur into a seamless panorama.

Moving forward into the living area, a U-shaped sofa invites relaxation and camaraderie, while cleverly housing a treasure trove of storage compartments beneath.

Beyond that, the kitchen beckons, with its thoughtful layout of a worktop with hob and sink down one side and a domestic-size fridge freezer on the other, to keep weeks' of fresh supplies. They have chosen to go without an oven, although this sacrifice is more than compensated by the ample space freed up to stash essentials and accommodate services, such as the boiler.

Next to the fridge is the main entrance door, with a wet room cubicle comprising a shower and toilet tucked in the corner beyond. High-level cupboards all around the ceiling maximise storage options.

In their pursuit of self-sufficiency during remote expeditions, the truck will be a marvel of engineering. To prepare for extended journeys off grid, they plan to carry 600 litres of diesel, two 20-litre refillable LPG cylinders for cooking and heating, and a massive 350 litres of water. Anti-bacterial filters allow them to refill from rivers and other natural sources, ensuring water sustainability.

Powering their expedition is an impressive 1,300 watts of solar panels, to guarantee energy autonomy, even in challenging weather.

Inside will be a haven of light and space, meticulously designed to subsume nature and connect with the outdoors. Two large double-glazed windows grace each side, allowing daylight to dance freely across the interior. Additional half-sized windows adorn each of the rear doors, framing the landscape. Three roof lights will punctuate the ceiling.

Together, these portals to the outside will flood the inner sanctum with light, creating a sense of openness and connection which transcends the confines of the truck's walls. The distinctions between indoor amenity and outdoor splendour will dissolve into a harmonious union. A celebration of the beauty that surrounds us, both inside and out.

In the world of Grand Designs, where each little detail is a brush-stroke on the canvas of innovation, Jackie and Mark intend to orchestrate a masterpiece within their compact abode.

If they can pull this off, this small space will be transformed into a symphony of storage, in which every nook and cranny sings with the harmony of practicality and purpose. Nevertheless, it's not merely utility that defines their creation.

In this paragon of practical mobile living, they intend to engineer an indoor/outdoor fusion and breathe life into a lustrous oasis, where functionality meets finesse.

Nonetheless, leaving the finer details and project management in the hands of the builder can be a risky proposition. While it's reasonable to entrust certain aspects to the professionals, ensuring a seamless execution often requires meticulous oversight and attention to detail. It's crucial to have a clear vision and maintain active involvement throughout the process to ensure that your dreams are fully realised.

Let's hope their decision doesn't lead to any unexpected challenges down the road.

Chapter 10

March – August 2020

Insulation

The first job was to insulate and line The Beast, but on the 11th March, the World Health Organisation declared a pandemic.

A week after Italy had locked down fully, the UK Government suggested people stopped non-essential contact and travel. Within days, Boris Johnson echoed my own misguided optimism and announced, "The UK can turn the tide of coronavirus in 12 weeks."

Seven days later, on 26th March, the UK went into coronavirus lockdown.

It lasted until June.

Other than one hour of outdoor exercise per day, essential shopping, seeking medical attention, caring duties, or work that couldn't be done from home, it was illegal to leave the house.

All non-essential businesses and shops closed, and police had powers to break up 'social gatherings' of more than two people.

The restrictions made sourcing materials for our build almost impossible.

Unexpectedly, what saved the day was the fact that our UK residence was falling down!

Hell hath no fury like a pack of petty pensioners. From our eyrie in the Italian Alps, we had to fight hard to enable essential roof repairs on our apartment building to proceed during the lockdown. It was a major project, which had to be done in the better weather and would take most of the summer. For urgent safety reasons, we couldn't put it off until the following year.

A small minority of our neighbours punched well above their weight. They were retired, and could have filled the twilight of their days with the peace, tranquillity, and beauty afforded by the semi-rural surroundings and the grounds of a former stately home. Instead, they sought ever more innovative ways to cause the maximum amount of trouble for those who had all the responsibility and work forced upon them: i.e. us.

They suffered an affliction that affects too much of humanity. Given paradise, they transform it into Gehenna.

When Mark and I purchased the apartment, we became one of the management company's eight directors.

"How hard can it be?!" we joked, not realising that unpaid, it meant we had omniscient responsibility for everything that happened on the estate. This included managing a Grade 2 star listed main building with eight apartments, plus ten acres of shared grounds which contained twenty-five freehold houses.

Our responsibilities involved mediating in all kinds of neighbourly bickering, from, "He planted a geranium a millimetre over the boundary of my freehold land!" (which we had no say over, because it was freehold) to "Please don't fire your air guns in the communal gardens.

In particular, don't dress your 12-year-old son in camouflage gear and instruct him to zig-zag across the lawn while you take potshots at him from your third-floor balcony."

Just normal, run-of-the-mill property management stuff, really.

UK Government guidelines encouraged the continuation of considerate construction. However, although our neighbours were perfectly happy to welcome the postman and delivery drivers right to their door, they objected to the proposed works on the main house on the basis of social distancing. Other than the gunman, the complainants did not live in or anywhere near the building in question. They rejected the argument that the contractors could easily maintain social distancing because they were working outdoors, on scaffolding more-or-less in the stratosphere, on a cordoned-off building, four storeys above a spacious, ten-acre estate.

They threatened a blockade!

Personally, I hoped their blockade proposed more adequate social distancing measures than when their ringleaders accosted the builders on the drive to quiz them about work on a property that did not even belong to them.

The contractor was a local firm, whose boss showed Mark and I his appreciation for our support by sourcing insulation and battens for The Beast.

In lockdown, the large roofing contract would keep his company afloat and his staff employed. A point dismissed by our delightful fellows. People's livelihoods were a piffling irrelevance compared to a chance to hide behind the mock outrage of danger to their persons. They could not pass up a prime opportunity to spoil someone's day.

Yet we knew them well enough to be certain that they would have deployed exactly the same mock outrage on the basis of negligence and danger to their persons had the same essential maintenance work failed to go ahead.

Secretly, part of me hoped that some masonry might fall on their heads to emphasise the point that it was 'essential maintenance'.

These charming, new neighbours made our hearts fill with gladness for our life choices. Our nomadic lifestyle grants the option to move on immediately if we don't like those around us.

With no immediate plans to move back "In The Brick," we remained optimistic. Hopefully, our dream home would return to its previous joyful state by the time we finished our travels. In those heady days before the new incumbents moved in, Mark and I used to organise cycle rides to the pub for our fellow residents. On sunny Friday evenings, we would meet up to drink wine on the lawn, or enjoy live music, and Pilates classes together, while raising money for charity.

Still, in this instance, their bad behaviour had really done us a favour.

To source battens and insulation during lockdown, all you need is a collapsing residence and neighbourly discord!

If you want the technical details of the insulation and how it was fitted, see Appendix 1.

Lining

Laminate to line the insulated interior walls proved more difficult, but Miles had a trick up his sleeve. With nearly fifteen tonnes of payload to play with, weight was never a consideration in our conversion.

"Stained wood will look great and be significantly cheaper than lightweight laminate," he told us. "Spruce ply has a terrific grain and takes stain well. You're looking at way over a grand (£1,000) for laminated panels, so this self-staining method will also save a few quid."

Miles promised a silky-smooth finish to the wall panels,

"They will be stained and varnished," he assured me.

That was a relief.

Dust traps are a pet hate of mine.

In the history of trends in interior design, I found louvre doors and plantation shutters particularly bleak developments. The ambitious array of solar panels we proposed for The Beast would generate sufficient power, but I couldn't imagine mustering the enthusiasm to vacuum the walls as we passed through dust bowls like the Gobi Desert.

As we had discovered in our rented Italian apartment, through months of cohabitation with 1980s hessian wallpaper, there is much more to life than hoovering walls.

Miles sent photos of various stained finishes. In the end, we opted for a pale turquoise paint wash for an 'underwater' look.

While the unexpected hurdle of a global pandemic causing shortages of materials meant the conversion was progressing more slowly than expected, something else cropped up that could require extra, unbudgeted work.

Miles told us, "Hey, I made a campfire last night by The Beast and heard some very strange noises. The usual contraction of panels as the day cooled down, but some clunking inside going on... I think the truck has a poltergeist!"

Maybe we would need to get a priest in.

Heatwaves & Headaches

Between March and May 2020, lockdown Britain enjoyed the sunniest spring on record. 'Furloughed' workers sunbathed, while the exchequer paid them 80% of their salary to stay at home.

On July 4th, the Government lifted most lockdown restrictions and urged people to return to work. They issued health and safety guidance on 'COVID Security', so businesses could operate safely.

On July 31st, the Met Office reported the UK's third hottest day ever, when it recorded temperatures of 37.8°C at Heathrow.

Throughout this spectacular summer, Miles filled his social media feed with seaside snapshots. His vibrant montages showed him with his kids at the beach, making the most of the heatwave. Mark and I were sanguine about it. After all, freedom and the flexibility to live in the moment were perks of his alternative lifestyle. He kept in touch about details of the build, and emailed the occasional photo, so we presumed everything was progressing as planned.

However, for us, all was not well in Europe.

After lockdown lifted in Italy, we'd spent the summer touring Eastern Europe in our caravan, dancing on the edge of uncertainty. Our route was dictated by dodging a coronavirus spike here, or an outbreak there.

In August, we were in Lublin, almost on the Ukranian border, about as far east as you can get in Poland.

There, global events finally caught up with us.

I shared the bombshell with Mark.

"The news says France is 'bubbling with coronavirus cases' and may be the next to come off the UK's safe travel list."

France was our route home.

It was not only a question of health. We had a deadline. Big Blue's MOT safety test ran out in six weeks. There had been an MOT 'holiday' during Britain's first coronavirus lockdown, but it seemed unlikely that the DVLA (Driver and Vehicle Licensing Agency) would grant a grace period now if we got stuck abroad. No MOT meant invalid insurance. No insurance meant illegal to drive. Plus, if the UK Government imposed quarantine on returning travellers, we had nowhere to go. We'd rented out our apartment to fund our travels, so we couldn't go back there. Although isolated and self-sufficient inside the caravan, we doubted any campsites would welcome a touring party fresh in from a coronavirus hotspot. Plus, if we had to quarantine, how would we exercise the dogs?

The following day, we started our race home.

We told Miles we were returning a month early from our travels.

"I've set August aside to really get stuck in with The Beast," he replied.

Initially, he'd said he'd have it finished by July.

We hoped his social media feed was merely a mirage.

Throughout August, with two months to our end-of-October completion deadline, it remained replete with sun-drenched shots of his endless summer.

Chapter 11
September 2020

181 Days Into The Build
Time to Completion Deadline – 8 Weeks

First Date With The Beast

"You don't realise how big she is until you stand next to her!"

Mark's words from his own first date with The Beast echoed in my mind when, for the first time, I did just that.

Mark is 6'6" (2 m) tall, so he already inhabits a super-sized universe. I'm a rather more diminutive 5'5" (1.65 m). Our new purchase, a faded NATO-green fortress-on-wheels, stood 13 ft (nearly 4 m) high. Her immense presence cast a shadow over me as she obscured the flawless cerulean blue of the first-of-September sky.

A magnificent bull nose towered above my head. As I gazed upwards, I considered the possibility of a new career as a life-sized model for Volvo N10 hood ornaments.

I pictured myself as 'The Spirit of Liberty'. A slightly dumpy female figure leaning gracefully into the wind, clad in a fleece and hiking boots, with four small fluffy dogs leaping at her feet as a roll of poo bags unfurled elegantly from her waist.

The N10's distinctive grille gaped like a portal to another dimension. A dimension that housed 9.6 litres of turbocharged diesel engine and delivered the power equivalent of 275 horses.

As I tiptoed around, I admired her robust exterior, composed of three rectangular boxes. Nose. Cab. Cargo area. She resembled a child's drawing of a lorry. Yet, her squared off edges and bold lines exuded strength and character. She had presence. A utilitarian, no nonsense industrial aesthetic that embodied the simplicity of Scandinavian sophistication.

Six heavy duty knobbly tyres, the height of my chest, raised her chassis 4 ft (1.2 m) from the ground. I photographed The Fab Four next to them. Their heads didn't reach the wheel hubs. "We can go anywhere!" the tyres screamed. "We mean business."

To one side of the four drive wheels at the back, I spotted a leaf spring.

I love a leaf spring.

I didn't know they existed until Big Blue's rear suspension collapsed because hers had rusted away. Ever since I discovered leaf springs, I've had a slight obsession with them. I often poke around chassis to check out other people's.

Leaf springs are simply a stack of flexible metal strips (or 'leaves') layered on top of each other. A simple and reliable type of vehicle suspension, unless they rust away, of course. But if you don't live on the coast, and don't fill your van full of sea water every weekend for a decade because it's your windsurfing bus, leaf springs provide years of support, stability, and shock absorption with minimal maintenance.

I gasped when I glimpsed The Beast's impressive undercarriage.

It was like catching sight of a purebred stallion at the peak of his fecundity.

"Mark. Look at *those*!" I blurted. "They're *twice* the depth of leaf springs I saw on that steam locomotive on the Swanage railway!"

To mount my metallic steed, I had to clamber up two steel steps, then use a huge metal grab handle to swing myself into the driver's seat.

Straight away, a symphony of scents hit me.

I adore the smell of old vehicles.

Classic cars, whose distinctive fragrance of worn leather, polished walnut veneer, and age, immediately whisk me off on a nostalgic journey back to an era of elegance, glamour, and craftsmanship.

Vintage planes, with hints of Bakelite, aviation fuel, and doped canvas, whisper tales of derring do. Their signature scent summons visions of dashing aviators in sheepskin jackets, advancing the boundaries of human achievement. Or steely eyed fighter pilots, who face danger head on, with laser-sharp focus, resilience, and honour. Triplanes, biplanes, or monoplanes: they are all filled with the intangible aroma of aviation's golden age. They speak of courage, exploration, and the realisation of Icarus' dream.

The Beast's own unique olfactory cocktail wrapped me in a comforting embrace of dependability, strength, and solid endurance. She exuded an aromatic miasma of ancient dust and elderly vinyl seats, with a hint of rust, bare metal, and old engine oil.

I ran my fingers over the dark textured plastic of her dashboard, greyed with thirty years of greasy, ingrained grime. Her dials and instruments were as pragmatic, functional, and down-to-earth as the rest of her. An analogue speedometer dominated the space behind the unpadded steering wheel. Stark white markings in km/h stood out against the black. A faded rubber gasket held in place the slightly fogged circle of glass.

No brass.

No chrome.

No hint of a decorative flourish.

Many fittings were lumps of unpainted metal with sharp edges.

Basic.

Unfussy.

Functional.

I still couldn't quite believe the odometer reading, which showed 5,703 km.

Despite three decades of military service, the several hundred kilometres from Rotterdam to Bournemouth was probably The Beast's longest ever drive, by far.

One rotary knob, which looked like something used to regulate the gas on a camping stove, caused an impromptu grin to spread across my face. A nod towards her military background, I felt a slight shiver of excitement when I realised twisting the knob let me select 'Standard Lighting', 'Convoy Lighting', or 'Total Blackout'.

The cab loomed above an ocean of detritus in Miles' yard, but the plastic palm tree, half empty paint pots, Calor gas cylinder, and discarded pink kiddie bike leaning on her front tyre somehow didn't detract from The Beast's majesty.

Her vast windscreen framed my view. It captured the horizon like an expansive glass canvas. Side windows and smaller panes to the rear flooded the cab with natural light, and granted me 360-degree visibility. Elevated way beyond the mundane world of hatchbacks and SUVs, I felt I was in a watchtower. I was a Trucking Belle, an Empress of the Road, surveying my asphalt realm from the protective sanctuary of an ivory tower, faced with steel.

The cargo box obscured my rear view, although the Volvo N10 tractor unit comes with a greater variety of rear ends than Kim Kardashian.

Should you choose to sculpt your *derrière* into a load-handling crane, a tipper, or low loader, instead of a cargo box, the N10's all-round cab visibility is a massive bonus

In the months to come, as we got to know The Beast more intimately, we would uncover many such thoughtful, user-friendly design features.

Next to the adjustable driver's seat was a bench wide enough to accommodate two passengers. Both were upholstered in mottled moss-green vinyl. I stroked the smooth, unblemished surface, incredulous to find no stains, cracks, or frayed stitching. The edges of the thin board that supported the ceiling head liner were disintegrating with age, but otherwise, The Beast showed no other signs of wear.

Once again, I grabbed the oversized handle to swing myself out of the cab. I took the two steps carefully, then jumped down to ground level.

With a flourish worthy of P.T. Barnum, host to The Greatest Show on Earth, Miles cracked open The Beast's rear barn doors for The Big Reveal.

The cavernous interior of our new home.

And the progress of the build so far.

A shiny silver tunnel of naked aluminium ribs led my eye to a section where Miles had affixed wooden battens to the ribs and fitted insulation between. He'd covered the front bulkhead with stained wood, where a few strands of wire dangled through from the solar panels, which were already in place.

"What do you think?" Miles asked.

"I love it!" I replied. "I love the machine. I love the colour inside. I love it!"

He beamed, then said, "How do you feel about fitting a sun terrace on the roof?"

"Um. That would be amazing," I said. "I saw a couple sunning themselves on a motorhome roof terrace on Lake Garda. But I'm not sure a sun terrace four metres up is practical with four dogs."

I didn't say it, but given the build was so demonstrably behind schedule, I wanted to focus on essentials.

Miles' promise to deliver by July was always ambitious, even without lockdowns and shortages of materials getting in the way. Now it was September, and The Beast wasn't even fully insulated and lined.

Suddenly, the magnitude of the project hit me.

The end of October, our deadline for completion, was only eight weeks away. We still had to build an entire interior, with a kitchen area, shower and toilet, fit the door, windows, electric, water, and gas systems – and get The Beast MOT'd and road registered.

That was our next hurdle.

And it involved the great unknown: government departments.

A Frigorific Fiasco

From the outset, we knew Mark, Miles, and I had lived in vastly different realms, but never saw this as a problem.

Mark and I spent our working lives as corporate soldiers, beating back assaults from ever-increasing targets and ever-decreasing deadlines. Sure, we'd enjoyed all the benefits – including the one that recruiters never discuss. Burnout.

That's what drove us to seek refuge in a simpler, more economical travelling lifestyle that we could sustain without working.

On the other hand, Miles, our free-spirited comrade, chose an alternative path very early in his career. Financially, it was more precarious, but gave him the freedom to choose when he worked, and take his kids to the beach whenever the sun came out.

Diversity is the key to a strong team, and for years, our bond of friendship had transcended our differences.

With a long timescale for our build, we had thought The Beast was the perfect project for Miles. Something he could fit around other jobs as he pleased, but guaranteed him income in quiet times.

However, in the epic saga of The Beast, once we arrived on the scene, the clash of worlds soon made an entrance.

Mark, the seasoned planner, had spent 32 years wrangling 300 staff, managing a multi-million-pound budget, and delivering complex projects. A strategic virtuoso, he once executed an overnight changeover of a national logistics operation so flawlessly that the Board saluted him. They named him the paragon of project management – until they conveniently forgot and handed him his long-service award.

The boot.

Or redundancy, as they called it.

Enter Miles, the emperor of nonchalance.

"Be cool. We can order things as we need them," he scoffed, tossing aside the concept of lead times as though they were rose petals at a wedding. Meticulous foresight was not part of Miles' world. In his carefree existence, such details were annoyances to be swatted away like flies.

This mismatch in planning philosophies would prove to be the red-hot chilli seasoning in the bubbling pot of chaos. But let's not stir too fast.

The inaugural clash unfolded over the matter of a fridge.

We wanted The Beast to have off grid capability for weeks at a time. So, we'd ordered the most capacious offering from Vitrifrigo's line of campervan fridge freezers. It was a 2-way compressor fridge, which ran from 12-volt or mains. As a former fridge magnate, I felt a compressor would maintain its temperature better than an ammonia absorption fridge, with no risk of leaking toxic ammonia gas. Our sleek, black chunk of Italian refrigeration technology was so vast, it had to be delivered on a pallet.

But in Miles' laid-back universe, the fridge had committed the ultimate sin.

"What're you ordering that now for?" he railed. "We won't need it for weeks and we'll have to store it. Bloody office workers..."

If we'd known quite how many weeks we would have to store it, we would have blanched, but we'll get to that.

On delivery day, we called Miles to remind him it was coming, and make sure he would be at the yard, since that was never a given.

"If you're not there," we said, "We can come over to accept the delivery."

"It's fine," Miles replied. "I'll be there all day." I could hear the grin in his voice. He didn't need to say it. "Bloody office workers..."

Even at this early stage, we knew Miles' version of "all day" meant between the hours of 10 and 2, to accommodate a strict schedule of school runs, a leisurely lunch, and marathon political debates on social media.

Mark and I were in Big Blue on our way to walk the dogs when the courier rang. Mark was driving, so I took the call.

The courier was struggling to find Miles' yard. He was trapped in orbit, like a confused satellite. The gravitational pull of the surrounding labyrinth of country lanes had caught him and would not let go.

"Where are you?" I asked.

"I'm on Orchard Lane."

"You're almost there, then. Look out for some farm buildings, opposite a white farmhouse. I'll ring and ask Miles to come out and give you a wave."

Simple. Or so I thought.

I phoned Miles and said,

"The courier's nearby. He's looking for the yard."

"I know," he replied. "I just saw him drive past."

"You what? If you can see him, couldn't you go out and give him a wa..."

"They always bloody do this. The postcode brings you straight here! Bloody idiots..."

As I explained before, Miles' postcode was a testy subject of ongoing controversy.

Miles insisted it was a failsafe navigational tool to his exact location.

Everyone else maintained it led to a small collection of houses about half a mile up the road.

Plus, his yard had no identifying sign. To anyone driving past, it was simply a tumbledown cluster of derelict-looking red-brick farm buildings. It didn't scream 'thriving hub of business and creativity'.

I pointed this out, then asked really nicely, "Couldn't you just pop down to the gate and give the guy a wave?"

But Miles was adamant.

"The postcode bloody does bring you here. I'm not doin' his job for him. Cor. There he goes again in t'other direction! Bloody idiot."

"But Miles, if this delivery fails, a redelivery will cost us £50. It will only take you a few seconds to walk to the gate and direct him in."

Next to me in the driver's seat, I could sense a distention in Mark's dam of diplomacy.

"It's only a few yards. Why can't he go to the gate and wave the courier in?" Mark snapped, as Miles piped up,

"He's in a blue truck. He's turnin' round again at t'junction and coming back!"

"Why can't he…" Mark growled.

"Mark, it's really difficult to hold a three-way conversation…Miles – PLEASE, can you…"

Mark's dam of diplomacy ruptured.

"TELL HIM TO GET TO THE GATE!" he yelled in my ear. I felt empathy with United Nations peace negotiators, trapped between warring factions.

"Miles. We offered to be there. We'd drive over now and wave the courier in ourselves, but we're fifteen minutes away. He'll probably have given up and left by then. That will cost us fifty quid. It's not far to the gate. Please, can you… Hang on. That's the courier ringing again…"

I hung up on Miles and gave the driver his final landing instructions.

It saved the delivery, our fridge-shaped dream, and a wad of hard-earned cash.

But victory came at a price.

Mark and I, the couple who never argue, found ourselves entangled in a post-delivery spat.

"Mark, it's really tough to be caught in the middle of a conversation like that. You know how difficult Miles can be. And with you both talking at once, I couldn't hear above the engine noise."

"You should have just told him!" he retorted.

"If I order Miles about, he *definitely* won't co-operate, and we can't afford to fall out with him."

Suddenly, a thought loomed large about the precariousness of our situation.

The Beast was huge, and she wasn't taxed, insured, or road registered. At work, as a manager, Mark could always fall back on hierarchy and procedures to resolve issues, but we were exposed. If Miles got angry and abruptly ordered us to get The Beast off his yard, what would we do?

"Do you remember what Roberto said?" I asked Mark.

Roberto, a dear friend, was CEO of a household-name company. He has exceptional skills in managing people and once, he told us his secret,

"You have to manage everyone differently, according to their personality."

In Miles' case, that resembled defusing a rusty, unexploded WWII bomb, ready to detonate without warning. With Miles, kid gloves weren't a sartorial choice, they were a wardrobe necessity.

Unfortunately, this tiff with Miles was a mere overture to a symphony of conflicts that would echo throughout our lives during the build, amplified by coronavirus lockdowns.

The Fridge became the unwitting opening act in a comic opera of missed deadlines, personality clashes, and the slow unravelling of the couple who believed they were immune to domestic disputes.

It was ironic.

A frosting of relations that would evolve into the most unexpected cold war since the Ice Age – and it all started with a fridge!

Iain

In late September, a spectral character with long-fingered hands became a more regular presence at The Vision Vault.

Iain, who also liked to be called Brian, depending on his mood, was a thin bowed figure whose lank black hair brushed the top of his collar. His pallid skin, rendered colourless by countless hours spent indoors, tinkering with tech, provided a stark backdrop for his dark moustache. If he possessed a shadow, it could have auditioned for the role of Nosferatu in a vampire movie.

His clothing consisted entirely of man-made fibres. Pilled black trousers, an inky monochrome acrylic sweater, and in all weathers, a short black coat with large square pockets at the hip. The only nod to nature in his attire was a slight grey-green sheen of dust or mildew on his coat, which he wore buttoned to the neck with the collar up to protect him from the battering rays of the sun.

Iain lived alone in a derelict horse box, abandoned at the end of a remote country lane. It was not road legal, so to get him to and from work, I became his unofficial taxi service. Wherever Iain went, he left behind a lingering aura of the kerosene he used in his van for heating and cooking.

The work Miles provided got him out, gave him social interaction, and a bit of extra cash. I thought he and Miles were long-standing chums, but Miles revealed he'd happened upon Iain, isolated in his horsebox, while out on a cycle ride with his girlfriend, Nicole, earlier that summer. They had chatted for a while, and Miles recognised Iain's potential. Miles was a master at spotting someone in need, then placing a solution before them with zero fuss.

Iain was a man of many talents, or so he told us. He was a qualified electrician and, although he didn't have Gas Safe registration, he could install our LPG system ready for inspection by a certified engineer.

He also said he had worked for a secure defence establishment, invented the CE Mark (which signals compliance with EU product safety standard), and single-handedly kept Britain's NHS (National Health Service) afloat during the 1980s.

On one journey, he revealed, "I made a crystal light up, just by holding it in my hand."

I must have looked sceptical, because he assured me, "That really did happen. It's because I'm a healer. I have power in my hands."

He got to work proving it with our pup Kai, who suffers from gastric problems. In the passenger seat, Iain placed his palms on Kai's tum and hummed. Kai did get better, but I can't vouch for whether it was because of Iain's healing hands, or the course of slippery elm and probiotics he recommended we try.

To Iain, work was even more of an abstract concept than it was to Miles, although he contributed to the sonic landscape of the yard with a ceaseless symphony of techno music he'd composed himself. Whenever he was there, a wall of white noise blasted out from the truck at a blistering number of beats per minute. Meanwhile, in total contrast, Iain moved and worked at a pace that could be comfortably mistaken for geological time. He often indulged in outdoor breaks, during which he'd wander around slowly, sucking thoughtfully on a vape. It took him a week to do a day's work.

Miles told us, "I'll deal with paying Iain, 'cos I know how much he's done."

Mostly, Iain did very little.

Conspiracy theories were Iain's bread and butter. Engaging him in conversation meant getting caught in an outlandish web of bizarre reasoning that could last for hours.

Once, while I was photographing the build and those who worked on it for my blog, he levelled a pale, bony finger at me and said, "You can't take a photo of me. I don't exist!"

Sometimes, he did things because, "Buddha told me to."

One day, as I drove him back from work, I could barely contain my mirth when he got out a walkie talkie. Via some advanced protection system of his own creation, he contacted his horse box by saying, "Calling home base. Calling home base." Presumably to unlock it and disable the elaborate security measures he'd brought over from the defence research establishment.

His dire financial straits were a frequent topic of his lengthy diatribes. Nevertheless, during lockdowns, he sported personal protective equipment appropriate for a fire fighter tackling a blaze at a toxic waste dump. He'd lecture me on the inadequacies of fabric face masks as a bulwark against coronavirus.

"They protect other people. Not you!" he'd complain from behind his reusable N95 mask, which conferred upon him the ominous wheeze of Darth Vader.

I didn't return the favour by lecturing him on how even an N95 respirator no longer offered protection once you'd touched it, exposed it to contaminated air, kept it in your pocket, or left it lying around inside your kerosene-infused horsebox.

Over time, we discovered Iain had a knack for extracting favours, and had a whole support network of people who pandered to him because they felt sorry for him. Iain managed his entourage like a string of affairs – none knew about the others!

Once, when I was driving him home, I encountered the lady who did his laundry. Each week, she drove two miles down the lane to provide him with a platinum standard collection and delivery service. She was on her way back because Iain hadn't bothered to be present to accept that week's consignment. When she passed a sack of freshly laundered, dried, and neatly folded clothes and bedding through her car window, he peered into it and said, "That looks okay."

Not so much as a hint of thanks!

Frequently, Mark provided lunch for everyone working on The Beast, buying burgers and bacon sandwiches from a van on the nearest industrial estate. Miles also kept Iain supplied with fresh water, allowing him to fill up his jerrycans at the yard. We drove them to his horsebox, and Mark carried them in, because Iain claimed he had a bad back and was unable to lift them.

Iain and Miles had an extraordinary talent for winding each other up. They fell out regularly. Every few weeks, they would have a flare up. Iain would quit in a huff, then Mark would spend a week trying to persuade him to return.

Occasionally, I ran into Caroline, who had been out in Italy with us, when she was out walking Oscar, her beautiful Spinone (a large Italian hunting dog).

Most people's lives trot along in a happy routine, but she was always eager to learn the latest drama in the bizarre comedy of our life.

"Last time we spoke, your electrician had walked out."

"Yes – he's gone again, and Mark's trying to convince him to come back."

Iain needed the stimulation, and we needed a gas and electrical system. As a condition of returning, Iain consistently demanded that Miles should apologise. Miles invariably refused, and insisted Iain must apologise.

Sometimes, Mark felt like chief counsellor to Tweedledum and Tweedledee. It took all his man management skills to tread the middle path and keep peace between the two.

When Mark came home, it was always dangerous ground for me to ask, "How was your day?"

It could go either way.

I could get a hilarious story, or unleash a frenzy of rage as the stress he'd been forced to suppress bubbled over.

One, "How was your day?" question revealed Iain's most spectacular meltdown to date.

"Iain's camera broke. He was inconsolable, so he left again."

"We don't use that old Olympus compact camera any more," I said. "We could give him that."

It wasn't the latest model, but it was a good digital device that took both stills and video.

Of course, Iain didn't proffer any thanks or gratitude, but thankfully, it coaxed him back to work.

Mark told me, "When I handed it to him, his face lit up like a child who'd seen Santa on Christmas morning!"

Iain used it to continue documenting the build.

Since Iain was on site much more than me, and was filming the project, I stopped taking so many photos. He was a tech geek and periodically showed us montages he'd compiled using the state-of-the-art media suite he kept in his horse box.

I was looking forward to the end result, but as with most things concerning The Beast, I could never have guessed the final outcome.

But more pressingly, with Iain in place to do the wiring, we had to make some decisions about the nuts and bolts of our electrical system. To help you understand our thought process, I'm going to introduce you to circuit training.

The Story of Creation (Batteries)

In the beginning (1799) in a laboratory far, far away (well, in Italy), Alessandro Volta and Luigi Galvani sparked up an argument about frogs' legs.

It would change the world!

Scientists do the strangest things.

Galvani had been busy prodding dissected frogs' legs with metal rods. He noted it made the muscles twitch. This, he asserted, was because they contained innate 'animal electricity'.

Volta was not hopping on board with Galvani's hypothesis. He believed the electricity was not inherent to animal tissues, but the result of contact between two dissimilar metals when they had some gubbins sandwiched in between. To resolve their potential difference, he devised his own game of electrical Jenga. He stacked up bits of wet cardboard with various metal combinations.

In one experiment, he assembled his signature Voltaic Pile.

He separated alternating layers of zinc and copper discs with sheets of card soaked in brine (salt water) to act as an electrolyte (a solution which conducts electricity). This simple arrangement produced a continuous flow of electricity and Watt's Up?

Volta had created the world's first battery!

This electrifying breakthrough sparked a whirlwind of discoveries in electrochemistry and electromagnetism. With not a trace of humour, scientists like Humphrey Davy developed huge Voltaic Piles and used them to create electrical arcs and isolate chemical elements by electrolysis.

Davy was the first to get his hands on pure potassium and unsullied sodium, as well as calcium, strontium, barium, and magnesium. All it took was zapping electricity (the electro bit) through molten salts or solutions. That caused them to split (or lyse) into their individual components at the electrodes.

Without Volta's Pile, Mary Shelley might never have written *Frankenstein* in 1816. And in 2020, Mark and I might not have been scratching our heads, wondering how best to power the electrical system inside our Beast...

But we haven't yet reached our full electrical potential.

In 1859, French physicist, Gaston Planté invented the lead-acid battery. Like Volta's Pile, Planté's setup also generated electricity from chemical reactions. But his genius discovery was that the process was reversible. When he sent a current through his contraption in the opposite direction, it converted electricity back into chemical energy.

Ohm my goodness.

Planté had created the world's first rechargeable battery!

Lead-acid batteries are still in use today, but a century on, not everyone embraced the idea of powering stuff with lead plates sloshing around in a lake of sulphuric acid.

Enter Gel and AGM (Absorbent Glass Mat) technology, which is rather reminiscent of the cardboard Volta used in his Piles.

Gel or absorbent fibreglass mats immobilise the electrolyte in contact with the metal electrodes, so it can't leak or spill.

It was one small, almost retrograde step for batteries, but a giant leap for anyone who wanted to corner sharply without splashes of acid melting their undercarriage.

A bonus for boy racers and fighter pilots everywhere, that's for sure.

But mankind is not a species to remain static.

While our quest for Olympic glory seeks 'faster, higher, stronger', in battery terms, it's 'lighter, more powerful, lasts longer'.

Enter lithium, the least dense metal of all. Indeed, it is the lightest solid element in the Universe, sitting third in the Periodic Table behind its gaseous cousins, hydrogen and helium.

Although they were all created in The Big Bang, lithium is rather less stable than its vaporous relatives. Because it reacts with almost everything, it cannot exist alone in nature.

Curiously, Robert Bunsen, of Bunsen Burner fame, isolated lithium from lithium chloride by electrolysis, the process made possible by Volta's Pile.

In 1976, more than a hundred years after Planté, British chemist Michael Whittingham patented the first viable lithium battery, using lithium metal as the anode (negative electrode).

Lithium weighs in at approximately one third the weight of lead. This meant his battery was light and powerful, but it had an irritating tendency to explode, for reasons I shall now explain.

When discharging (i.e. powering things), lithium ions dance happily from anode to cathode to generate electricity. The problem came when charging reversed the flow and deposited the ions back on the lithium metal electrode. These grew into tree-like metal fingers or 'dendrites'. If these became long enough to touch the cathode, they short-circuited the battery and created their own Big Bang.

In time, Whittingham's team got over this by 'intercalating', or reversibly inserting, lithium ions into carbon-based substances, such as graphite, instead of using lithium metal. This meant the ions were available to perform their electrical wizardry, but lived safely intercalated in little caves, like reef fish hiding among the coral.

Subsequent developments in materials improved the performance, stability, and safety of these lithium-ion batteries.

In the 1980s, John B. Goodenough at Oxford University made groundbreaking advances using cobalt oxide (CoO_2) as a high-energy cathode (positive electrode).

Scientists have since discovered other compounds that can store lots of lithium ions with minimal side reactions. The specific battery chemistry you use depends on the application. You might find lithium cobalt oxide ($LiCoO_2$) keeping your phone or laptop alive, or lithium manganese oxide (LMO) in your power tools. While lithium iron phosphate ($LiFePO_4$) has a lower energy density (energy to weight ratio), it is renowned for safety and long life, which makes it the darling of energy storage applications such as leisure batteries for recreational vehicles...

Which brings us back to The Beast.

We had a decision to make.

Lithium or AGM?

***

Everyone was talking about lithium. It was the new big thing.

Lithium has a longer lifespan than AGM, charges more quickly, and has a higher energy density, i.e. more energy in a smaller, lighter package. There is also more useable energy, since lithium batteries tolerate a greater depth of discharge (DoD) than AGM without risking damage to the battery.

As an example, a 100 Ah (Amp hour) AGM battery will deliver 50 Ah, while lithium might give you 90 Ah.

But there were some disadvantages. A lithium setup is more complex, requiring battery management systems and specialised charging equipment. Plus, lithium batteries are more sensitive to temperature extremes – AGM performs better in cold temperatures, which was a consideration for using The Beast as a ski bus.

We had some safety concerns about fire risk. Transportation authorities classify all lithium batteries as a hazardous material. This could mean logistical challenges should we ever wish to ship The Beast to another continent.

At the time of our build, AGM was a substantially more budget friendly option, but this was not the reason for our choice.

Our greatest concern was KIS.

Keep It Simple.

AGM battery technology is familiar territory.

Cars and boats have used them for years, so mechanics and engineers understand their operation and maintenance. They are also widely available, which could make them easier to replace, particularly in remote or developing countries, where lithium may be unknown.

We bought six AGM batteries, rated at 720 Ah, which would deliver around 360 Ah of useable power. This was a substantial amount, sufficient to give us hundreds of hours of LED lighting, recharge our phones thousands of times, and keep our fridge running for several days without needing to charge our batteries. With 1300 watts of solar on our roof, we thought this was a pretty robust system.

The Electrical System

'Buy Cheap Buy Twice' is an epithet to which Mark and I have long subscribed. We'd made it clear to Miles that our philosophy for the build was that, while we didn't want to throw money away, we didn't want to scrimp. We were happy to spend in areas where it would make a difference. This was, perhaps, at odds with many van life self builds, where budget is paramount.

Mark and I established that Victron was top-of-the-range for solar control systems, but Miles wasn't a fan. Possibly because they are as princely in cost as in performance. However, Miles also had his own merry band of favourite suppliers. Despite extensive research, solar power was still tantamount to sorcery in our minds, so we relied on his superior knowledge.

Once we'd purchased a well-reviewed solar controller to manage the energy input into our batteries, Miles emailed us a variety of eBay bargain accessories.

"This is a 5000-Watt pure sine wave invertor. Pure sine wave!" he enthused.

An invertor converts 12-volt power into 220-volt, so you can use regular household appliances. Some ladies favour an invertor capable of powering a hairdryer. Personally, I stick my head out of the cab window while we're driving, but 5000 watts would enable us to run power tools and a powerful domestic vacuum cleaner. An important consideration when you have four dogs in tow.

From Miles' reaction and a bit of research, I fathomed that pure sine wave was A Good Thing. Certainly, it was less likely to damage sensitive electronics such as our laptops. I bought it, along with an unbranded battery charger he recommended, to top things up when we had shore power (a mains electrical hook up).

In pursuit of resilience, we considered a battery-to-battery charger, which uses power from the engine's alternator to charge up the leisure batteries as you drive. We thought it would be a useful backup when we had insufficient solar power coming in, or no access to shore power to charge us up.

Miles dismissed it as surplus to requirements.

"1300 watts of solar up top. You could power a rock festival! You don't need that."

This, along with Iain's insistence that we didn't require a battery monitor to show the state of charge (or depth of discharge), was the direct opposite of inbuilt resilience.

Excessive charging or discharging of AGM batteries significantly impacts their capacity and lifespan.

Frogs or no frogs, it can make them croak.

Chapter 12

October 2020

211 Days Into The Build
Time to Completion Deadline – 4 Weeks

MOT Misery

My clothes smelled of diesel, my stomach churned, and my knuckles were white. For the first time, I heard the roar of The Beast.

I'd had a sleepless night at our campsite in Verwood. Storm Alex had raged around us, shaking Caravan Kismet and pounding her roof with torrential rain.

Worry Number 1 was that Big Blue would be so bogged down on the already sodden grass next to the caravan that we wouldn't even be able to drive to The Vision Vault to collect The Beast and escort her to her MOT – her mandatory roadworthiness test that was the key to getting her road registered.

Worry Number 2 was that a violent storm was hardly ideal weather for Mark's first outing in months at the wheel of an unfamiliar LGV.

The Beast was parked ten miles from our campsite. A few days prior to our appointment, Mark had messaged Miles to say, *Can you put The Beast's battery on charge?*

Miles forgot. So, when Mark dropped in the previous day, he couldn't check she'd start.

Although Mark covered it with a bin liner, Worry Number 3 was that beneath the Biblical deluge, the battery charger would have failed in its duties overnight.

To our relief, on the first turn of the key, The Beast thundered into life.

"We need to get some air into the brake system," Mark explained as she ticked over, filling the yard with her muscular growl and a cloud of blue smoke. I gave voice to Worry Number 4.

"You won't run out of fuel?" I asked, well aware of her hefty usage, even as she idled. I recalled that when Mark brought her back from Rotterdam, €250 of diesel had not even cajoled her gauge out of the red – and that was several hundred miles ago.

With 24-volt electrics in the cab, Worry Number 5 was that our 12-volt satnav was useless. This left me and Big Blue with the job of escort vehicle, to lead The Beast's 24.5 tonne majesty to one of the few garages in the area able to service an LGV.

We had booked The Beast in for seven days of mechanical pampering and pre-MOT checks. This, we hoped, would coax her through her first MOT test. Coronavirus was on the rise. We wanted to get her registered as soon as possible, in case another lockdown closed down public services once again. But first, we needed fuel.

Miles warned us not to rely on the satnav down the narrow warren of farm tracks that surrounded his yard. He gave us directions for a suitable escape route.

"Agricultural vehicles go down there, so you'll be fine wi't' truck," he assured us.

I was less confident.

In my discombobulated state, by the third junction, I had forgotten the directions. *Was it the first or second right that led to the big roundabout on the main road?*

Mark was piloting The Beast. He was relying on me and I was lost in a maze.

At the end of the lane, I came upon a route that I knew led to the roundabout.

It was ninety-degrees left with a width restriction.

I panicked. *I don't think she'll get through…*

My snap decision was to turn right, with butterflies in my stomach, no idea where I was or where I was going, and with a huge army truck in pursuit.

Although I had programmed in The Beast's weight and dimensions, the satnav disagreed vociferously with my re-route. It tried to lure me back on track via a housing estate. It was only when I turned in, I realised parked cars obstructed the street on both sides. Luckily, Mark was far enough behind to spot me in the process of executing a hasty U-turn and had the sense not to follow.

Eventually, I emerged on a small back road I recognised, so I stuck with it. With my windows down, I could hear the mellow rumble of nine-point-six litres of power behind me. I also overheard many a "WOW!" as our strange motorcade passed through the winding lanes and thatched villages of rural Dorset.

My target was a fuel stop on the main dual carriageway. It was not the cheapest, but I knew The Beast's 3.85 m elevation would fit beneath the canopy with no need to duck.

Once we arrived, my frayed nerves needed a hug from Mark – and a Snickers bar to boost my blood sugar. The Beast needed two £100 diesel injections to get out of the red. £100 was the maximum the pump would allow, so I had to go inside to pay each time Mark hit three figures.

Had we filled both tanks to the top, we may have been some time.

We continued on to Blandford at around 40 mph, to the accompaniment of enraged hoots from ill-tempered motorists on the dual carriageway. One bloke sliced in front of me with inches to spare as the road narrowed from two lanes to one. He failed to see the irony of shaking his fist at me as he mouthed something slightly ruder than, "Bloody women drivers." I wasn't the one driving dangerously!

The truck garage was in the middle of nowhere.

Although Mark and I had done a reconnaissance trip the week before, I missed it on my first pass. I had to proceed two miles on the country lane to a roundabout where The Beast could turn around. All I thought about for those four miles was, *That's cost us half a gallon of fuel!*

It was a relief to reach the garage safely. I felt totally drained, but that wasn't the end of the story.

"Where's the paperwork?" Phil, the engineer, asked cheerily as he booked us in.

"What paperwork...?" Mark replied.

Eight months previously, the DVLA (Driver and Vehicle Licensing Agency) returned our registration application and told us we needed to MOT The Beast before we could register her.

That seemed odd, so Mark questioned it.

"We've imported a vehicle from abroad and you're saying DVLA doesn't need to have it on record to apply for an MOT? I would have thought it was logical to register it first, before the MOT."

The DVLA assured Mark this was not the case.

When he asked if there was anything further he needed to do to smooth the path to MOT and registration, a decisive answer came back straight from the horse's mouth.

"No."

This was, of course, entirely wrong – or entirely right, depending on your point of view.

DVLA had discharged their responsibilities.

However, there *was* something we needed to do with the DVSA (Driver and Vehicle Standards Agency) and they didn't mention that.

In a sentence that caused our blood pressures to soar and our morale to plummet, Phil told us,

"You need a VTG1 to get the MOT, mate!"

The MOT was just a week away. How would we do that?

At the best of times, public services are notoriously slow, but during the pandemic, government departments did not share the country's enthusiasm for remote working to keep business ticking over during lockdown.

Then, over the summer, when Britain's illustrious Prime Minister encouraged furloughed staff and home-workers to return from beach to office, the DVLA remained resolutely closed. The only way I could contact them was via Facebook. When I messaged to ask when they might re-open, they replied helpfully,

"We cannot provide a timescale."

A week's insurance cover to drive The Beast to the garage had cost £200. Plus, with the post-lockdown backlog, the likelihood of getting another truck MOT date soon was as slim as Mr. Slim of Slim Land who had just been named Slimmer of the Year.

Phil raised a few more potential issues that might scupper The Beast's chances of passing her MOT.

Although she was incapable of speeds above 50 mph (around 80 kph), even with a following wind, she needed a speed limiter fitted. An almost impossible feat on a truck of her vintage.

The Beast's tyres looked new and unworn, but planned legislation required tyres on the steering wheels of some vehicle types to be fewer than ten years old. It wasn't yet in force, so we hoped it wouldn't apply.

However, the MOT required a brake test laden. Phil said the test centre had concrete blocks to simulate a load, but loading was not really an option, because of The Handbag Theory.

This is my hypothesis that, however big your handbag, you will fill it.

Miles was a perfect exemplar of The Handbag Theory.

His yard, workshop, van, and two storage trailers were all rammed to capacity with tools, bits of wood, metal, various building materials, junk that might come in useful one day, and junk that definitely wouldn't.

The Beast's arrival provided a monumental amount of additional dry storage. Admittedly, for many necessities required by our build, but it meant she arrived for her MOT full of spruce ply, insulation boards, a pallet with our fridge strapped to it, and a varied collection of tools and other random detritus. We could have removed some of it, but there was far too much to fit into Big Blue.

Utterly demoralised, we surrendered The Beast to Phil and left.

A few days later, we were even more dejected.

Mark took Big Blue for her MOT.

We made every effort to ensure she would pass. Painstakingly, we burnished her rheumy headlight lenses with toothpaste, checked all her bulbs, and had replaced her sagging and rusted leaf springs. Yet we still had some nagging doubts as to whether she would make the grade.

Mark drove to the Hyundai garage and surrendered our beloved van to her fate. After an anxious sixty-minute wait in reception, the engineer came out and handed him Big Blue's keys.

"We don't do van MOTs. Bye!"

Mark reeled for a second, but he was not taking that one lying down.

"What?!" he demanded. "We've had this MOT booked in with you for eight months. You've serviced and MOT'd this vehicle before. You're a Hyundai dealer and you're telling me now, after an hour, you didn't know this Hyundai iLoad was a van?!"

Seemingly not.

The engineer was unsympathetic and unapologetic.

Big Blue was our only transport.

At the weekend, we had to move the caravan from Verwood because the campsite was full.

In a couple of days, when her MOT ran out, Big Blue would be illegal to drive.

Verwood was in the sticks, with no mobile signal or internet connection, so from the reception at the Hyundai dealership, Mark made frantic phone calls around the counties of Hampshire, Dorset, and Wiltshire, and tried to arrange a short-notice van MOT.

"Sorry mate, can't do anything for at least three weeks!" was among the best answers.

Thankfully, persistence and pleading secured a test at 9 a.m. the day the MOT expired. The day we had to move our caravan off the campsite. We just had to hope and pray Big Blue would pass.

Against all expectations, she did.

A week later, after moving Caravan Kismet to a new location on Calshot Spit, near Southampton, we were yet more jubilant. I said to Mark,

"Is our run of terrible luck changing?"

In our wildest dreams, we didn't imagine that The Beast would pass her MOT first time.

Without the VTG1, we hadn't believed we could enter her for an MOT. Much telephone wizardry and some string pulling by Phil's extensive contacts squeezed out an emergency VTG1 in a matter of days.

Surfing our wave of success, we tried once again to register the truck.

Our paperwork arrived with the DVLA in Swansea just as Wales went into a second coronavirus lockdown. Still, they found just enough time to reject it.

Despite a metal plate embossed with '1990' spot-welded onto the chassis, plus a manufacturer's certificate of conformity from Volvo in Sweden, DVLA cited 'insufficient evidence of the year of manufacture'.

If we couldn't road register the truck, it was game over for our project.

***

The Belgian army had bought The Beast in 1990, as the Cold War was ending. With fewer than 5,000 km on the clock, she'd clearly spent her life in strategic storage, before being decommissioned without distinguished service or honours at the tender age of thirty.

Her Majesty's Revenue and Customs had been swift to pop out of COVID hibernation to note her low mileage.

"If the mileage is under 6000 km, the vehicle is considered new," they declared. "As such, VAT (Value Added Tax) at 20 per cent applies."

"We paid VAT at 21 per cent in the Netherlands when we bought her," we argued. "We were assured that, since the UK is still effectively part of the EU, we would not need to pay VAT again when she was imported into the UK. The truck was manufactured in 1990. She's 30 years old. She's anything but new!"

Out of interest, we asked Miles to check The Beast's odometer. The journey from Belgium to Blighty had taken her mileage to... 5703 km. Our 30-year-old spring chicken was 297 km short of being considered 'not new'.

The potential tax implications associated with each one of those 185 miles made her disastrous fuel economy look like the bargain of the century!

We'd just had the double whammy of losing more than a month's rent and being forced to pay for alternate accommodation for our tenants due to a fire in a neighbouring apartment that was not our fault. A demand to hand over a second fifth of the purchase price in tax set us on yet another novel and completely-impossible-to-predict collision course with Financial Armageddon.

But the challenges didn't stop there.

Now, besides a hefty unexpected tax bill and failing to get her road registered, the world was an entirely different place from when we'd bought her in January, with Mongolia in our sights.

The earth was in the throes of a global pandemic, during which domestic and international travel became illegal.

Countries we planned to drive through were in turmoil. There were riots in Georgia, conflict in Nagorno-Karabakh between Azerbaijan and Armenia, and Belarus descending into a Russian-backed dictatorship, to name a few. Combined with the devastating economic impact of coronavirus on the poorest countries, the most optimistic prognosis was that the world order would only get more unstable.

It made us wonder whether, for the second time in her life, The Beast was destined to become a white elephant.

Post MOT Blues

October turned into a month of missed deadlines.

Mark assessed the tasks yet to be completed and emailed Miles a summary. It made depressing reading.

I was just thinking about what needs to be done on the truck and what I still need to buy. It seems a lot of work for an end of October target. Do you think that's realistic?

We need to buy & fit*: door; windows; roof lights; fresh water tanks; purification system & pump; accumulator tank; shower, basin; pipework for water & grey waste; lighting; sockets; toilet; black waste tank; hob; LPG heating, hot water and gas plumbing; external spotlights; reversing camera.*

We need to make and fit*: steps; gas bottle storage box; interior cupboards and framework; interior soft furnishings; rear bike platform.*

Miles' reply was prompt and succinct.

You have too much time on your hands. LOL!

It was reassuring to know he took our predicament so seriously.

Slowly, the realisation was dawning: simply expecting your mate to act reasonably does not a contract make.

***

October, supposedly a month within the season of mists and mellow fruitfulness, was as uncooperative as Miles. At least as far as the weather went.

Undeterred and keen to make progress, Mark tried to gird Miles into action via email,

Weather crap. We'll keep an eye on it. Monday looks like a bit less rain and Wednesday looks good. Would suggest Sunday, but it looks just as sh**ty.

Again, Miles's reply was prompt and to the point.

I don't work weekends. LOL.

The end of October was patently not realistic.

We extended the deadline to the end of December, hopeful that Mark and I could capture the ski season from January onwards.

Halloween Horrors

But another curve ball soon looked like it might jeopardise our deadline when news reports began to mention a new, highly mutated coronavirus variant. Circulating in England's south eastern county of Kent, it was 30-50 per cent more contagious than the original strain, and more likely to land victims in hospital.

For the second year in a row, Boris Johnson, Britain's Prime Minister, had a Halloween fright. The previous year, 2019, he neglected to find himself 'dead in a ditch' on failing to deliver Brexit as promised on 31st October.

For weeks, he had ignored government scientists' pleas for tougher restrictions, and insisted another lockdown would be 'disastrous' for the economy. His chief advisor reported Johnson as saying, "Let the bodies pile high."

But when infection rates and hospitalisations surpassed even the worst-case scenarios, Johnson called a hasty press conference.

On 31st October 2020, he admitted, "We've got to be humbled in the face of nature."

He announced a second four-week coronavirus lockdown, starting from 5th November. Pubs, restaurants, and non-essential retail would close once again. Overnight stays and travel, local or international, were banned.

Shortly before, on 28th October, France had already entered its second nationwide lockdown in response to a record number of infections recorded in a 24-hour period.

Even if we had completed our build by our end of October deadline, we couldn't have gone anywhere.

Grand Designs Revisited

The Grand Designs programme format always includes an interim sum up, so I shall hand you over to virtual Kevin for his assessment of our progress so far:

As October unfolds, it reveals a deluge of dashed hopes for Jackie and Mark.

Miles' optimistic projections, promising completion by July, soon unravelled. The shadow cast by the pandemic rendered July's goal more ambitious. Yet, by the time August transitioned into September, The Beast lacked even the basics. Although she sports a fine array of solar panels, her interior remains a barren canvas, devoid of insulation and lining.

Now, as international borders close and another lockdown looms, Jackie and Mark's attempts to get her road registered have failed.

Ever the diligent planner, Mark meticulously outlined the tasks still to be completed, presenting Miles with a sobering reality check. His cavalier dismissal is a stark reminder of the precarious nature of reliance on verbal agreements.

In this ongoing saga, it's becoming clear: optimism alone cannot forge a path forward.

We find ourselves grappling with the harsh truth that expectations, unanchored by contractual clarity, are but a fleeting whisper in the wind.

Back in the Brick

One piece of good fortune in October was that our tenant moved out of our apartment.

In the previous lockdown, campsites had closed. If that happened again, we would have nowhere to pitch the caravan.

With no idea whether the government would extend November's lockdown, we decided to move back 'In The Brick'.

This gave us the chance to experience the exact reverse of the usual Grand Designs scenario.

From the comfort of a cosy apartment, we could observe a half-built mobile home surrounded by freezing mud and construction chaos.

Although one thing I couldn't say about the apartment was that it was cosy.

Since this was Lambertshire, returning to our residence would never be straightforward.

After many heartfelt discussions, Mark and I reluctantly concluded that paying to store the caravan while living in our apartment was a waste of money. The decision tugged at our heartstrings.

Caravan Kismet was more than a mobile home. She was our faithful companion, our cosy sanctuary, our ticket to freedom... For four glorious years of Adventure Caravanning, she'd carried us safely through ten countries, braving rivers, mountains, and even the odd footpath as we tackled some of the world's most dangerous roads.

But alas, the call for cash to fund our build grew louder.

With heavy hearts, we bade farewell to Kismet and committed to The Beast.

It felt like abandoning an old friend.

However, selling Kismet burned our boats somewhat.

In the summer, we had turned our backs on our nasty neighbours. Tired of the never-ending melodrama, we had sold our apartment. The sale was due to complete in November, by which time, The Beast was supposed to be ready.

No problem, we reasoned. *If we can't move into The Beast, we can find somewhere to rent.*

If only things were so uncomplicated.

We searched in vain for somewhere else to live.

As landlords, we had always welcomed furry friends, but even we might have baulked at being asked to accommodate four. Plus, coronavirus lockdowns had stalled the property market. In such a period of uncertainty, nobody was on the move.

Our honest admission that we came with a quartet of well-behaved, non-shedding dogs meant we plummeted to the bottom of every landlord's and agent's dream tenant list faster than you could say, "muddy paw prints".

Fortunately, our buyers, Pamela and Alan, numbered among our genuinely nice neighbours and we had become friends. We could not in good conscience have dumped our embattled dwelling on to some poor unsuspecting victim. Pamela and Alan knew the score.

They had bought our apartment as a rental investment. In the circumstances – impending lockdown and looming homelessness – they graciously agreed to let us stay on as sitting tenants in our former home.

They even settled on a gentleman's agreement to rent it back on a monthly basis, without the usual fixed six- or twelve-month commitment of a Standard Assured Shorthold Tenancy.

Stupidly, Mark and I still believed the world would open up, that The Beast would be ready in a few months, and we would be able to travel once again.

Domestic Violence!

Pamela and Alan's kindness made it all the more painful when, days after the apartment officially became theirs, it staged a rebellion.

First, the shower stopped working.

Then, in the icy grip of a brutal cold snap, the central heating went on strike.

Had we been the homeowners, we would have speed-dialled Andy, the plumber who fitted the system for us. Part of me was still eager to do that and just pay to get it fixed. At least that would save the embarrassment of Pamela and Alan thinking we'd kept the issues quiet until the sale went through.

But as tenants, protocol dictated we must contact our landlords.

Pamela sent in Chris, her own plumber, who replaced the shower mixer. After several wallet-wearying visits, however, he left us with nothing but chills and a sense of mortification, which grew exponentially with each guilt-wracked call.

"The heating's still not working..."

Even when Chris fitted a new central heating controller, it made no difference.

Then the toilet started steaming.

Its cistern was filling with hot water!

I had a long conversation with Pamela and suggested she summoned Andy. Chris was good, but didn't seem to understand our particular model of boiler.

"On the last visit, he called the company's support," I told her. "But it's still not working."

My stomach churned with disquiet as Andy diagnosed both the boiler and the hot flush problem in seconds.

"There's a reset button on the boiler. See that red light? It's lost communication with the controller. You just need to press it."

"So, um, we didn't need to replace the controller?"

"No…"

As for the hot flush, there was good news and bad news.

"It's a valve underneath the bath that has failed. I'm not even sure why it's there. It's a historic house, so it must relate to some previous setup."

That was the good news. The bad news was horrific,

"The only way we can get to it is to take out the bath…"

I could have cried when I told Pamela, because by that point, the oven had started to fuse all the electrics each time we switched it on and the shower door had fallen off its runners and needed replacing.

The only saving grace was that we would have sorted all the problems out before 'proper' tenants moved in.

Embarrassment meant we were exceedingly tolerant of three weeks with no heating, no shower, no oven, and flushing the loo with a bucket. Guilt compelled us to be understanding about wearing fleeces indoors, huddled around our hearth, and hanging around to host a revolving door of maintenance visits.

Goat Curry

Before lockdown restrictions came back, one of my favourite aspects of the build were the cook ups we had around the campfire, which was a permanent fixture at the yard.

Miles used the fire to distress wood for his artistic creations, but gastronomy was his other passion. So, as evening fell, he regularly repurposed it in pursuit of edible art.

Food tastes better cooked with flames, and Miles was a genius at conjuring all kinds of exotic flavours from them. Frequently, he would turn dinner into a social event, and share it with others in the van life community.

Mark and I often brought over a chicken. As he did with driftwood, Miles's eyes would light up as he imagined what he could create.

"I'll spatchcock that, wrap it in foil on a bed of preserved lemons, stick in my special spicy sauce and leave it to roast slowly in the embers."

Sometimes, he'd use a homemade oven he'd crafted from a pair of wheel hubs welded together. When this curious contraption sat amid the coals, it spread the heat to ensure everything cooked through perfectly.

Once, he announced he'd make a campfire cake in his own inimitable way.

"Two stainless steel dog bowls – one pound fifty each at Milford Supplies. Clip 'em together with bulldog clips. Flour, eggs, nuts, and sugar. Mash up a banana. Mix it up. Shove it in t'coals. Ten minutes. Perfect."

It wasn't perfect, partly because Mark had been at the campfire. Mark is the embodiment of 'Man Make Fire'.

He loves a bonfire and could never help piling on an extra log – or twenty. A lacework of small holes ventilated most of Mark's best fleeces, melted by sparks from one of his mega conflagrations.

"Tell 'im to stop puttin' wood on there!" Miles would rail at me. "I need it to die down for t'cooking. And I'll be 'ere 'til midnight waiting for that to go out."

When he removed the bulldog clips and split open the dog bowls on to a plate for the big reveal, it was impressive. An external torus of carbon encircled a liquid centre of raw cake mixture.

Yet between the two was the Goldilocks zone. A narrow strip of fluffy sponge, which would have been perfect, apart from one thing.

Miles grinned as he tasted it. "I forgot the bloody sugar!"

Heavily influenced by his time in Morocco, Miles's signature culinary speciality was goat curry. Whenever he could get the meat from a specialist butcher hidden somewhere out in the sticks, he'd suspend his huge cast-iron cauldron on a tripod over the fire and we knew we were in for a treat. He'd call everyone up, and we'd all gather around to enjoy tender, slow-cooked goat in his own thick and spicy North African sauce.

I enjoyed our campfire chats.

For Mark and me, it was a window into a different life. We come from a very middle-class background, but that didn't seem to matter. Everyone made us welcome, and we found it liberating to move in circles where how much we earned, the seniority of our jobs, or the size of our house or car didn't define our worth as people. We were just Jackie and Mark with the truck and four dogs. It was refreshing to find acceptance based on your deeds, and how you behaved towards others, rather than the meaningless trappings of wealth.

Miles was an unerringly generous and charming host. In his understated way, he supported the community. Anyone could come to his yard to use the space, his expertise, and his tools to work on their vans. He trained up youngsters, quietly providing paid employment, teaching them skills, and giving them somewhere to be.

After one cook up, we'd eaten all the meat from the goat curry, but there was plenty of sauce left in the pan. Unasked, Miles put it into a container, handed it to a guy called Cliffe, who lived in the back of an estate car with his dog.

"Tell you what. Get a tin of baked beans. Rinse off all that 'orrible tomato sauce, then heat them up in this. Bit of rice. You've got a delicious dinner," he said.

I'd just had the most humbling conversation with Cliffe. He'd told me,

"I love these cook ups. I don't take food for granted, you know. Well. Because it's not always there..."

His comment hit me like a battering ram. It shattered the door of my perception and opened it up to a new landscape of understanding.

No, I thought. *I absolutely do not know.*

Even as an impoverished student, there has never been a day in my life where three meals were not a given. Sure, I ate a lot of eggs and baked beans, which were cheap. But unbeknownst to me, my parents had guaranteed me an overdraft with the bank. Whenever I went to see the manager, Lem Jones, I wondered why he was so amenable. His kind face would beam at me like a benevolent uncle, with his hands clasped as he leaned on his dark mahogany desk. Then, in his sing-song Welsh accent, he'd ask,

"Now, my luv. How much mun-nee do you need?"

I never pushed it and invariably asked for a modest amount.

Sometimes, he'd say, "Now. Are you sure that's enough? You have your rent to pay. And your bills."

But whatever the sum, he always said, "Yes."

I had guardian angels.

In life's lottery, not everyone is so fortunate.

Chapter 13

November 2020

242 Days Into The Build
Time to Second Completion Deadline – 8 Weeks

Skylights

"I t's good news!" Miles grinned proudly as I stepped carefully around a lake of water on the floor inside the truck. "T'skylights aren't leaking. That's condensation."

I didn't feel it was cause for celebration, but Miles's tone made it clear. He'd discharged his responsibility. Leaking was his bag. Rivers of condensation from our newly installed custom designed skylights was an issue for Mark and I to resolve.

We were already way behind schedule with a mountain to climb with respect to the build. The slightest disagreement with Miles always carried the risk of an eruption and a downing of tools. He'd fixed in the skylights. There was nothing to be done. It brought to mind an old prayer.

God, grant me the serenity to accept the things I can't change,
The courage to change the things I can,

And the wisdom to know the difference.

Displaying a modicum of serenity and wisdom, I smiled and remained silent.

Four solar panels occupied most of The Beast's roof, so Miles had designed and fitted the three long thin skylights into the narrow spaces in between.

The splendour of this unusual architectural feature thrilled virtual Kevin McCloud, and Miles was delighted with his efforts.

"Look how much light they let in!" he enthused. "Even when we cut t'hole for the first one, it was like turning on floodlights."

The ghost of Miles past echoed in my head. *It'll look good for t'photos, but nowt will work.*

Miles had insisted on non-opening skylights because, "With t'movement of the body panels, skylights ALWAYS leak."

Skylights usually sit proud of the roof. If they're sealed in properly, I saw no reason for them to leak. I had been quite keen on having opening skylights. Hot air rises, so they punch above their weight in terms of ventilation as well as illumination. Ironically, this would also have helped dispel the condensation... But the long, thin shape of our skylights, dictated by the space between the solar panels, did not lend itself to opening.

Later, I had to face the eruption on the home front.

"Why is there condensation on the skylights when they're double glazed?"

"But they're not double glazed," I told Mark. "The fabricator fitted two panes of security glass in each of them, but there's no gas-filled cavity between them, so there's no insulation."

There was no point arguing – the expensive custom skylights were bought, paid for, and irremovably sealed into the body of the truck.

We would have to live with them and find a solution.

I could almost hear virtual Kevin's soliloquy about overseeing the design of essential components, rather than entrusting the fine detail to someone you think will know better than you.

***

The skylights were the first substantial openings we'd made in the truck's body. As singer Rod Stewart observed, *the first cut is the deepest...* It was a nerve-wracking day.

"Will the truck be strong enough to support holes for all these windows, skylights, and a door?" I'd asked Miles.

"It will be fine," he assured me.

The Beast's body is formed from thin aluminium sheets, reinforced with box-shaped ribs every fifteen inches (40 cm).

I am the daughter of a bridge obsessive. I grew up with a framed photograph of the Humber Bridge in the hallway, a model Forth Rail Bridge to play with, and annual trips to North Wales to marvel at a multitude of crossings, including Robert Stephenson's Britannia Bridge across the Menai Straits.

As such, I am no stranger to the engineering merits of a box girder.

In box girder terms, Stephenson was an early adopter.

Structurally, his Britannia Bridge is basically one giant box girder.

With a continuous span of 1500 ft (461 m), when it opened in 1850, it was the world's longest bridge by a factor of 15.

For 120 years, it also reigned supreme as Britain's most easily maintained railway bridge until a fire in 1970 destroyed the original structure.

Initially, Stephenson recognised the immense strength, even load distribution, and resistance to bending and twisting of hollow iron tubes at Blackwall, London. In 1842, he witnessed the troubled launch of a steamship, The Prince of Wales. As she went down the slipway, her bow jammed on the wharf, while her stern wobbled around in the water. Stephenson noted that a hundred-foot-long section of the ship remained suspended in the air, but did not buckle.

If box girders are good enough to support distressed steamships, Stephenson's Britannia Bridge, and the Millau Viaduct, currently the world's highest, they're good enough to hold up The Beast's roof, adorned with four weighty solar panels when we cut great chunks out of her side.

At least, that's what we had to hope!

Steps & Bike Platform

In a similar way to getting the quad in and out, the steps to access the habitation area posed a conundrum.

With the floor nearly 4 ft (1.2 m) above ground, we needed a stairway to heaven. Somehow, we had to grant access to our stratospheric front door for ourselves and four dogs.

The height meant there was plenty of space under our chassis. In cahoots with our welder, Jake, Mark came up with an innovative design for fixed steps built on to a hinged L-shaped frame that would simply pivot in and out from beneath the chassis.

Because of the height, the steps would be very steep. To combat this, the design evolved. They would add an extra slide-out step in the truck's body, directly beneath the front door. Then a sliding mechanism would allow the steps on the frame to pull out once folded down, which would reduce the gradient.

A significant advantage of the concept was that we could fold the steps in from inside the truck, which was not an option with most other designs. This was great for security, because it was akin to pulling up a drawbridge. If we were stealth camping, it would make us look less like a camper, and in narrow spaces, there was no chance of our steps getting hit and damaged by passing vehicles. Plus, the void behind the steps was a neat storage area. Our cupboard-under-the-stairs was so voluminous, we could consider letting it out to an orphaned child wizard.

However, as with any new and innovative design, it took a great deal of tweaking to get the details and the angles right.

***

Having abandoned the idea of a quad, we opted for bicycles as our runaround mode of transport, and wanted to build a platform at the back to carry them. In the spirit of 'you can never have enough storage', we thought we might as well make it into a storage box.

Jake was a lovely guy, against whom the Universe seemed to have conspired. Tragically, his wife had passed away suddenly, so he was a single parent looking after two kids. He'd lost an eye in an accident, and had endless troubles with his own van conversion.

The designs and welding all progressed smoothly until Jake sent us an apologetic email to say he was teetering on the verge of a breakdown. We told him not to worry and take whatever time he needed.

We still hope he's okay.

Although we sent a few supportive messages, he closed down all his social media accounts, and we never heard from him again.

Coronavirus Update

Mark and I spent the first coronavirus lockdown marooned in Italy. There, the rules were much stricter than those in the UK. We were locked down in a remote ski village with only half a dozen occupants. Our nearest neighbour was a national park and the second highest peak in Europe. Still, the regulations insisted we did not stray beyond the bounds of our garden. Road blocks and regular police patrols kept a keen eye open for infringements, with the *carabinieri* ready to slap a €1,000 fine on anyone who dared to transgress.

When we experienced the UK's second lockdown in November, the situation was considerably more relaxed. The government urged the nation to stay at home, with exceptions for a limited set of reasons. These included going out locally to shop for food and essentials; outdoor exercise with your household, support bubble, or a single person from another household; and work for those industries unable to do so from home, such as construction.

Infection rates were low in our region. It was easy for Miles, Iain, and Mark to socially distance as they had access to a large yard, a massive workshop, and the interior of our capacious Beast, whose rear barn doors could be flung open to keep fresh air circulating. We felt it was safe, legal, and moral to continue with our build. When I drove Iain to and from the yard in his toxic waste respirator, with an empty mate's seat between us, I shivered as I kept Big Blue's windows open for ventilation as an additional precaution.

With Mark at The Vision Vault every day, I walked the dogs alone at our nearest beach.

It was anything but relaxing.

A furloughed nation had been snapping up 'pandemic puppies' as companions. Prices rocketed, and some reports suggested over seven-hundred potential buyers clamoured for each advertised puppy.

Dog thefts soared.

When a television programme hailed Cavapoos as 'the perfect dog', they shot to the Top of the Pups as one of the most popular and desirable breeds.

During our Italian isolation, The Fab Four's antics and *joie de vivre* had rubbed off on us and kept our spirits buoyant.

Back in Blighty, I feared for my fur babies, with their fluffy coats and cute teddy bear faces. I could never relax.

In addition, as if I needed reminding, the dystopian sight of four abandoned cruise liners moored offshore in Christchurch Bay attested to the seriousness of COVID. They were a dispiriting shrine that encapsulated 'the new normal', where everything sort of looked the same, but could not have been more different. Life as we knew it had come to a halt.

Our local beach, Hengistbury Head, is my favourite place in the world.

Despite the variety of walks – from the harbour to the beachfront, through the dunes on a boardwalk, past the lily ponds in the woodland, or over the headland with its breathtaking views, going there started to feel like Groundhog Day. For months, every day was the same. I felt huge sympathy for those stuck in cities and recognised I was far luckier than most to live in such a beautiful place. Even so, the monotony and the solitude became overwhelming, and the stunning scenery was always overshadowed by crippling fear for the safety of The Fab Four.

But with a half-built truck making such slow progress, it didn't appear that my routine would change any time soon.

A welcome variation was that occasionally, I ran into Caroline and Oscar.

The dogs always found each other – sometimes Rosie would run half a mile to greet her pal. Other times, a liver-and-white head the size of a rugby ball would nuzzle into my hip, and I would know Caroline was not far away.

Stuck at home during lockdown, most people's lives were on hold.

When Caroline and I walked together (two metres apart for social distancing!) I often left her open-mouthed when she asked how things were going in the freakish soap opera that was our life.

In November, my summary was,

"We're a month behind schedule, with no end in sight, so we've had to rent our own house back from our buyers. The house is possessed. The shower and central heating won't work, the oven fuses all the electrics, and the bath had to come out to stop the loo filling with hot water. Our welder has walked out, leaving our steps and bike platform half finished. Our skylights are wringing with condensation, which we've no idea how to fix. We ordered the windows, but they could take up to 12 weeks to come, but that doesn't really matter. Now it's winter and the weather's bad, we can't be cutting holes in The Beast. Plus, Miles said he has to halt progress on the truck because he wants to make some stock to sell for Christmas.

"Other than that, everything is hunky dory. How are things with you?"

Chapter 14

December 2020

302 Days Into The Build
Overrun – 1 Month
Time to Second Completion Deadline – 4 Weeks

Coronavirus Update

I n case you forgot how scary it was, on December 3rd 2020, the global coronavirus death toll passed 1.5 million.

In the UK, government statistics stated the virus had claimed over 60,000 lives: one of the highest mortality rates in Western Europe. As an advanced island nation, that seemed particularly appalling, but things were about to get worse.

The high infection rates gave the virus plenty of opportunity to mutate, or evolve, to up its game. By December, the new, more transmissible Alpha variant from Kent, in southeast England, had really taken hold.

Europe placed travel restrictions on countries with the highest levels of contagion. This included the UK, Turkey, Iran, France, and Sweden.

To control the spread when they lifted November's lockdown, the government introduced tiered restrictions. The severity varied according to local infection rates, but it meant more than half of England could not mix indoors.

Outdoors, the 'rule of six' applied – no more than six people from two households could meet socially.

Even so, the new variant ripped through the British population.

Boris Johnson's response was to lambast those who called for another lockdown. In mid-December, at Prime Minister's Questions, Johnson accused the opposition leader, Sir Kier Starmer, of wanting to "cancel Christmas!" He assured the country there would be no lockdown until the new year.

On the 19th December, three days later, Johnson changed his mind. He forbade Londoners from leaving home and banned all mixing between households. Elsewhere, a maximum of three households could meet indoors, but only on Christmas Day.

Since the rules in London didn't come into force until two days after his announcement, news footage showed a mass exodus from the capital via public transport. This meant they could spend Christmas – and export the disease – to places where the restrictions were less onerous, where the Alpha variant could spread unchecked.

Of course, Johnson didn't apply his own rules to himself.

The subsequent Partygate scandal not only suggested that Downing Street held several raucous Christmas parties during December's lockdown, but also that the Johnson family were kind enough to host a guest at home on Christmas Day, despite the ban on household mixing.

mRNA & A Lesson in Immunology

At least December brought a glimmer of good news.

On the 8th, 90-year-old Margaret Keenan became the first person in the world – outside a clinical trial – to receive Pfizer-BioNTech's newly approved messenger RNA (mRNA) COVID-19 vaccination.

Margaret signified the start of the largest mass-immunisation campaign in the UK National Health Service's history. Health and social care workers, along with those over 80-years-old, were vaccinated first. After that, the programme rolled out to other groups, prioritised by age and their susceptibility to severe illness or complications from COVID-19.

As a former research biochemist, the mRNA vaccine excited me.

To explain why, I need to give you a brief lesson in immunology!

Your immune system is your body's bouncer. It keeps out unwanted gate crashers such as viruses, bacteria, and other pesky pathogens. It's a smart system that learns to recognise troublemakers by their distinctive external features, known as 'antigens'. When it spots an antigen it doesn't like, it whips up a custom-made storm trooper, or 'antibody', with special powers to disable that intruder and quickly show it the door.

Vaccines act as boot camps for immunity. They use either the real deal with its hands tied behind its back, or lookalikes, to train your body to fight off the baddies. Traditional vaccines introduce an antigen to prep you for the genuine article. Think of it as showing your immune system mug shots of germs, with instructions on how to kick them out quickly, often before anyone notices the ruckus.

But mRNA vaccines are different. Although it is a genetic material, mRNA cannot alter your DNA. (DNA is your fundamental genetic blueprint). mRNA is just a type of customised memo, written in the body's own language, which tells your cells what to do. Your DNA usually issues the memos, but an mRNA vaccine impersonates them. It instructs your cells to whip up a specific mug shot, such as the infamous spike protein on the coronavirus. As soon as it does, your body's defence system spots the intruder. It then gears up a new team of carefully primed bouncers, who stand ready to bar the door if any lookalikes turn up.

Since an mRNA inoculation doesn't contain any actual virus, just its mugshot, there's zero chance of you catching the disease. Plus, like most memos, it soon ends up in the bin as your cells break it down. Your immune system is the one who remembers the intruders.

The body uses mRNA (messenger RNA) constantly. Without it, you wouldn't be alive. An mRNA vaccine is essentially a flight simulator, which trains your body's natural defences while eliminating the risk of a crash.

But the massive game-changer is that mRNA vaccines are like having your best Savile Row tailor on speed dial. Compared to guessing which strain of flu might be fashionable the following season, then waiting all summer to grow it in chicken eggs or some such, mRNA can deliver bouncers briefed in the latest flu fashion from lab to nightclub in double quick time. If the virus suddenly decides a mutation into *trompe l'oeil* detailing and rainbow stripe socks will help it get in, a few tweaks, and mRNA will be there to escort it from the premises.

Yet, despite all this high-tech wizardry, the government announced that those, like us, in the lower-risk groups would have to wait almost a year to get our COVID shots. The much talked-about vaccine passport seemed aeons away. Foreign travel, a distant dream.

As an over-50, however, I was well up the list for receiving a seasonal flu jab. Unfortunately, that didn't go quite so swimmingly.

The second the nurse put the needle into my shoulder, I felt a squelching sensation spread into my neck.

It wasn't the vaccine: I think she hit a nerve.

For the next three months, I had a frozen right shoulder.

The Window Seat

In our apartment, the mobile phone only worked right next to the small sash window in the hallway. Because of the thick stone walls, the sill was just deep enough to sit on. This allowed you to rest your head on the glass – the only position with sufficient signal to hold a conversation. Turn your head, and your conversation ended.

In the spring of 2021, I spent a lot of time in the window seat.

One reason was physiotherapy.

My flu jab left me with a frozen shoulder. Face-to-face medical consultations were suspended because of coronavirus. My doctor made her diagnosis over the phone, asking me to perform various range-of-movement tests. She referred me to a physiotherapist, who posted me a set of resistance bands and a printed sheet of stretches. The physio scheduled weekly telephone appointments to give me new exercises and check on progress.

I'm not entirely sure what the neighbours made of my antics in the window!

***

The other thing that tied me to the window seat was Stuart.

One of the more challenging aspects of our travels the previous summer was launching an international missing persons hunt from Berlin.

Our dear friend Stuart rang us at 4 a.m. one morning, after an earlier conversation in which he'd told me,

"I'm thinking of taking loads of pills and alcohol and ending it all."

Stuart's cosy, happy life had shattered when his long-term partner left. Shortly after, he received a diagnosis of an aggressive, incurable cancer and tragically lost his mum, all while in the midst of relocating to a new, isolated rural home as the UK entered its first coronavirus lockdown.

After treatment, he became a walking miracle and tested fully clear of the cancer. However, he knew no one locally, had no support network, and was so terrified of contracting coronavirus, he refused to leave the house.

Mark and I were fast asleep when the call to Berlin came in the wee small hours. By the time we'd leapt out of bed and found the handset, the phone had rung off. We called back straight away, but there was no answer. We redialled several more times, but he did not pick up.

Throughout the day, Stuart's phone immediately switched to answerphone. In desperation, we phoned his local hospital to see if he had been admitted. He hadn't. At that point, we felt there was no choice but to call the police – not easy when you're outside the UK, I can assure you. The emergency numbers don't work from abroad, and neighbourhood police stations no longer have direct contact numbers.

After being bounced around switchboards for hours, we eventually spoke to someone who agreed to send an ambulance to do a welfare check on Stuart.

I experienced conflicting emotions shortly afterwards, when an indignant Stuart finally called to demand,

"Why on earth did you call an ambulance?"

"You rang us at 4 a.m. and we've not been able to contact you all day. After our conversation yesterday, you must understand we were really worried," Mark explained.

His reply was as unexpected as it was bright and breezy.

"Oh. I was tired because I'd been up all night. I turned off my phone so I could get some sleep."

Back in Blighty, as Britain entered its second, then third lockdowns, I sat for many hours in the window seat with my head pressed against the sashes, offering pastoral and other support to Stuart. He rang three times a day, which made it difficult to get anything done. No sooner had I finished my morning call, than it was time for our midday chat. Making conversation was a struggle. I tried to be upbeat and did not discuss our problems, but once I'd covered Stuart's daily highlight, which at best during COVID, was ironing his trousers, there wasn't much else to say. Often, I spent ages reassuring him: "Your tests show your cancer is in remission. It's unlikely you've contracted COVID because yours is a very low-risk area. Plus, you've had no contact with anyone because you never go outside."

Stuart was not computer literate, so I collected a weekly list from him to do an online shop, which was delivered to his door. He wore a mask to accept the delivery, and sanitised everything before he took it into the house.

Because he was bored and lonely, Mark and I also ordered a smart TV with a Netflix subscription for him, to give him access to a wider choice of entertainment on demand.

It turned into an IT support nightmare, not least because we're hardly IT brainiacs ourselves.

He struggled even to use the TV remote. Fortunately, the TV we sent him was the same as ours, so we could view our own controls while talking him through the instructions. Nonetheless, he'd argue vehemently that the buttons we asked him to press did not exist on his handset.

"There is no x for escape button. Look, I'll read through all the buttons to prove it. 1.2.3...8.9. Oh. x!"

We dispatched a simple MiFi internet hotspot unit to him, and told him it had to be switched on if he wanted to watch films on Netflix.

"There's only one button, right in the middle. To turn it on, press and hold the button. When the green light is on, it's working. A red light means it has no signal, and yellow means the signal is poor."

"It's not working!"

"Did you press and hold the button?"

"Yes. It came on and switched off again."

"Ah. You need to press and hold until it comes on, then let go, otherwise it will switch off again."

"Oh, okay."

"Is it on now?"

"Yes."

"But it's gone off again."

"Hold the button, but not too long. Is it on now?"

"Yes."

"What colour is the light."

"It's white."

"It doesn't have a white light. Is it pale yellow?"

"No. It's definitely white."

I tried not to sound exasperated.

"Oh, well I suspect it is yellow, so the service isn't good. You need to put it somewhere so the light turns green."

Since Stuart's signal was almost as bad as ours, the phone would often cut off at this point because he'd moved.

We tried to be patient when he deleted all the passwords because, "It wasn't showing the password. It was just a load of dots in a box." Sometimes, he got so frustrated with our IT support that he'd hang up on us.

But eventually, we got him on Netflix, for part of the time, at least. Until he plucked up courage to seek support elsewhere. At his local mobile phone shop, he bought himself another SIM card for the MiFi unit because it was much cheaper.

"It's only £6 a month!" he gloated, and all but accused us of ripping him off.

The new SIM card didn't work, because it was calls and texts only. It didn't have data.

Lesley

In addition to coronavirus lockdowns causing a shortage of materials, many other factors conspired to slow down our build.

Besides contending with Miles' brief working days based around childcare, political rants, and lunch breaks, Mark was never certain he would be present at the yard.

Communication was difficult.

Miles blamed us, but tracking his availability was a military operation reminiscent of monitoring aircraft movements during the Battle of Britain.

Miles's messages could appear at any time of day or night. They might arrive as texts or WhatsApps on either of two mobile phones, as messages on any of three email accounts, as comments on random threads on social media, or via Facebook Messenger.

At home, our phones were rarely about our persons. They usually languished in the hallway window, the only place in our apartment with a signal, which made it easy to miss the demanding ping of a message notification. Mark and I had never mastered using email or social media on our mobiles. These days, the expectation is that people pick up notifications immediately, but with us, instant messaging was anything but, because it had to wait until we switched on our laptops.

The Vision Vault was a fifteen-minute drive away, or more if Iain needed collecting en route. Often, Miles' messages arrived after Mark had left in the morning.

Miles berated us both constantly.

"Check your messages!" he'd email, text, WhatsApp, message, comment – or yell, on the occasions when we actually met face to face.

I admit we are technological dinosaurs, but the poor phone and internet signal at The Vision Vault added a whole extra layer of confusion.

Sometimes, Miles' messages sat in his outbox for days. Frequently, Mark turned up to find the yard deserted. If he called to see where Miles was, he'd get a, "Check your messages!"

Or Mark stayed at home because Miles had said he wouldn't be there – but the message was from two days previously. Then he'd get a call to say, "Where the f@*! are you?"

On the occasions when they did converge to work on the truck, the first half of Mark's day inevitably involved running around Screwfix, Toolstation, and Milford Supplies to acquire the drill bits, screws, hacksaw blades and whatever other materials were required for that day's tasks. Occasionally, Miles sent him further afield, such as to Southampton, a 45-minute drive each way. Once, Miles dispatched him there in the morning to source wood. Then again in the afternoon to buy metal.

When Mark was held up in traffic on the second return journey, Miles' demand, "Where've you been for that? F@*!ing Mongolia?" did nothing to assuage the tension.

One Monday, however, driving to Yeovil to rescue a baby squirrel was not how Mark intended to spend the day.

Mark and Iain were out on the regular DIY shop rounds when they spotted the kit in the road. Her mum was nowhere to be seen, and a car had run over her sibling. She was uninjured, but terrified. When Mark picked her up, she grabbed the end of his finger. They bonded instantly!

Mark phoned me and drove her home so I could meet her. She stayed in Big Blue on Iain's lap. It was clear he was very taken with her. He cradled her so gently, wrapped in Mark's down jacket. She was jumping with fleas. Systematically, Iain removed and crushed them between his finger and thumb.

"I've called her Lesley," he told me. "Because that can be a boy's or a girl's name."

While waiting, I had contacted the local vet, an animal charity, and wildlife rescue. All gave the same response.

"We can't take grey squirrels. They are an alien species in the UK. Because they're classified as a pest, it's illegal to release them into the wild. All we can do is put her to sleep, I'm afraid."

We couldn't let that happen to Lesley!

An internet search turned up Acorn Squirrel Rescue, a dedicated centre based in Bristol. When I called, they were very enthusiastic about taking her.

"Squirrels are such wonderful creatures!" Anne enthused.

Since Acorn was two-and-a-half hours away, we agreed to meet in the middle, in Yeovil.

When I saw her, Lesley was very relaxed, curled up and sleeping, but the boys said that, en route to the rendezvous, she nibbled on some broccoli, cauliflower, and carrot.

That evening, we called Acorn to check on Lesley. Anne told us,

"She's settled in really well. Although she was hungry and dehydrated when she arrived, she took some milk and more vegetables. She's recovered enough to go in with a little friend, so she won't be lonely after losing her sibling."

Lesley had found a home for the rest of her life.

While she could never go back into the wild, we were happy she now had a comfortable and contented future.

We hoped the same might apply to us.

If we could just get this truck of ours finished...

The Best Christmas Present Ever

Brexit was looming.

On December 31st, Britain would leave the EU.

We didn't know what implications that would have, because details of the 'Oven Ready Deal' were yet to be announced.

Still, just before that auspicious date, we got the best Christmas present ever.

Not only did HMRC (Her Majesty's Revenue and Customs) surprise us by conceding that our thirty-year-old vehicle was not new, and waived their claim of an additional twenty per cent Value Added Tax. On Christmas Eve, after Volvo in Gothenburg intervened with yet another small but very significant piece of paper, we received a letter from DVLA.

The Beast, a Belgian army lorry that had never been road registered, finally gained British Citizenship as a private LGV.

Mark and I celebrated, albeit our elation was short-lived.

Travel restrictions were in place all over Europe, and with a week to go to our second completion deadline, she was as near to complete as Boris Johnson's fabled 'Oven Ready' Brexit Deal.

Chapter 15

January 2021

332 Days Into The Build
Overrun – 3 Months
1 Day After Second Completion Deadline

New Year, New Start?

J anuary didn't start well.

On the 1st, as we roared into the Roaring Twenties, Johnson's 'Oven Ready' Brexit deal, which had morphed into an impending 'No Deal', became the hardest of hard Brexits.

Then, unsurprisingly, after transporting the virulent new coronavirus variant across the country over Christmas, January was the UK's deadliest pandemic month to date. On the 2nd January, the UK COVID-19 death toll passed 75,000. The government announced a third national lockdown, starting on January 6th.

***

A hard Brexit meant Britain disengaged fully from the European Union (EU), leaving both the single market and customs union. This raised a trade barrier the size of the Great Wall between them.

With Britain finally free from the shackles of EU controls and red tape, the understudy, British red tape, stepped in. Importing anything from Europe now involved enough of it to tie a bow around the moon.

Travel-wise, a ferret with a Romanian pet passport had greater freedom of movement than a British citizen. As did The Pawsome Foursome. They had French pet passports, so they could still travel freely, but in an area that encompassed nearly thirty European countries, we could only accompany them for three months in every six.

Unfortunately, Britain's newly regained 'sovereignty' also impacted travel to other destinations whose visa agreements were with the EU, not Britain. This included Russia's 'E' visa.

Russia was a major part of our route to Mongolia.

Mark and I soon noticed the immediate Brexit benefits.

More duty, more VAT, more shipping costs, more admin costs, slower delivery – and exorbitant fines for companies who got it wrong.

We fell foul of Brexit in our attempts to purchase electric bikes, Sikaflex adhesive, and Savoy cabbages!

When we abandoned the idea of a quad bike, we considered a motorcycle or scooter. Online, we were enamoured with a vintage BMW bike and sidecar combo that had taken part in the Paris to Dakar Rally.

"The seller said it would be perfect for us," I enthused. "It's similar to The Beast - built like a tank and can run on any rubbish kind of fuel. And the sidecar is so cool. It would be great for the dogs. The downside – it's heavy and bulky. Same as the quad – it will be just as difficult to transport..."

Despite the glamour of a former Paris-Dakar combo, common sense prevailed. It wasn't solely that the Silver Machine was too cumbersome, and a bike without a sidecar was useless for transporting The Fab Four. Mark and I had to admit – we were too irresponsible to own a motorcycle.

Mark has only ridden a motorbike twice in his life. Thankfully, only ever in fields, because he crashed on both occasions – once in spectacular fashion. He overcooked the throttle, launched at speed into a wheelie, toppled over sideways, then slid the bike beneath a barbed wire fence in full Steve-McQueen-in-the-movie-*Great-Escape* style.

For years, I'd terrified myself commuting to work in East London on Mike the Bike, a Honda 50 moped. I worked as a beer taster at a brewery, which afforded me some perks. When I loaded my free monthly allocation of three crates of Budweiser on the back, Mike became erratic and almost impossible to control. The slalom through rush hour traffic on Westminster Bridge was an adrenaline ride unlike any other.

When I moved out of the city, I persevered with my Biker Chick journey on a Suzuki 125. However, after too many near misses, I felt certain that one day, the actions of a careless motorist would mean I lost the use of my legs.

Or my life.

So, I abandoned my motorcycling career.

In the end, we opted for electric bikes equipped with the doggie trailers we already had to fit our mountain bikes.

We scoured Britain online. There wasn't a single electric bike for sale.

Partly, that was down to the pandemic. A glorious summer plus a population paid to stay away from work meant an explosion in the popularity of cycling. However, a local cycle shop yielded another, somewhat bleak, Brexit-fuelled explanation.

"Customs impounded our last shipment because we got the paperwork slightly wrong. The fine cost more than the value of the shipment. So, we're not getting any more in."

When you consider that each electric bike costs several thousand pounds, that was an eye-watering penalty for a small business to swallow.

We experienced similar issues with the Sikaflex adhesive required to anchor our windows in place. Nowhere had any in stock.

Most companies said, "We've suspended imports."

The only supplier we could find was prohibitively expensive. It was easy to check how much Sikaflex cost in Europe. Import duty and delivery costs literally doubled the price.

After weeks of searching, we found a company who discovered a few tubes of Sikaflex292-i, the exact type we needed, lurking at the back of their warehouse. I had to pay £260 for 6 x 300 ml of glue, and 1 x 250 ml bottle of Primer-206 G+P. We couldn't source any Sika Cleaner 205.

Our Sikaflex was so rare and valuable, we collected it in person. I went along with Mark for the ride. As I waited in the car park, I saw a campervan with *"Dream higher than the sky and deeper than the ocean"* emblazoned on its side. I loved it, but it gave me a pause for thought.

Was our dream too ambitious?

Would it ever be realised?

At least compared to Britain's elite: privately educated politicians, who had made such a lash up of the two once-in-a-generation challenges of Brexit and a global pandemic, our performance looked relatively competent.

Britain had the highest COVID-19 death rate in the world, empty supermarket shelves, and huge gaps in the labour force because all the unwelcome immigrants had gone home.

The shortage of truck drivers was such that Mark received a government call up because he held a valid lorry licence.

Your Country Needs You, !

I, on the other hand, couldn't book lorry lessons or a truck test, because there was such a backlog as a result of coronavirus.

News reports showed queues of lorries who had drivers sitting at the Channel ports, awaiting customs checks. Those departing British shores were full of festering fish. Those eager to enter were replete with rotting produce – hence the dearth of Savoy cabbage.

Imagine that.

No cabbage. Right in the peak of an annual highlight: the winter casserole season!

Of course, the end of December was not only the Brexit deadline.

It was the third deadline for our build.

And we'd missed it by a spectacular margin.

During December and January, we made very little progress with the truck. When we finally laid hands on our Sikaflex, the instructions stated, 'The minimum application temperature is 10°C, but ideally 15°C.'

Rare enough during a British summer, but highly unlikely now it was winter. Not that it mattered terribly. Our windows wouldn't arrive for months.

We rehashed our timeline once again and begged for an extension from our landlords.

Pamela and Alan took pity on us and said, "Yes."

We decided to be kind to ourselves and settled on 1st May.

More than half of the seven-month timeframe we had initially proposed for the entire project.

Surely, we could achieve that.

Chapter 16
February 2021

364 Days Into The Build
Overrun – 4 Months
Time to Third Completion Deadline – 3 Months

The Door

The door was an example of when tomorrow comes several months late.

A few weeks earlier, well, eleven to be precise, Miles said to Mark, "Order the door and we'll fit it tomorrow."

Mark did as he was told, but had to urge Miles to be cool when he broke the news that 'tomorrow' couldn't happen for two-and-a-half-months, because of a small thing known as a ten-week lead time.

When the door finally arrived with the supplier in February, its two panes of security glass didn't, which delayed us another week.

Miles's unpreparedness for this delay was all the more surprising, since it was he who gave us the details of a local company he'd used before. They supplied secure front doors for houses.

At least Miles' recommendation had solved the conundrum of what to do about an entry door for the truck.

From bitter experience, we knew that standard RV doors were not remotely secure. Thieves demonstrated this neatly when they forced open our caravan door with a screwdriver.

We had qualms about the durability of a horse box 'groom' door, while the specialist 'overland' entry doors were shockingly expensive. Besides being costly, something custom made would probably have delayed the build even longer.

A standard domestic-type security door struck a good balance between cost, protection, and quality.

Since The Beast is left hand drive and we spend most of our travelling time abroad, we installed the door on the right hand, 'European' side.

When I turned up at the yard to collect Mark in the gloaming of DFD (Door Fitting Day), his and Miles' progress wowed me. After waiting almost a quarter of a year for our door to arrive, I expected great things, but the vision that confronted me surpassed all expectations.

A large, rectangular orifice gaped in The Beast's side. Its upper quadrant revealed the top of the box containing our fridge, still enthroned on its pallet inside the truck. Miles' van, reversed tight up against the opening, was all that provided overnight security and weatherproofing for the truck's interior. Besides the state-of-the-art campervan fridge that had cost £1,200, The Beast contained a tempting and highly portable cornucopia of tools, solar components, and valuable building materials, all of which would turn a great profit when sold online.

As an afterthought, as Mark and I drove off, Miles wedged an insulation panel into the gap above the roof of the van to complete the weatherproofing and security arrangements.

On this occasion, my, "How was your day?" question didn't cause a detonation, but it yielded an interesting answer.

"The process of converting the truck's side from a wall into a hole was fairly quick," Mark explained on the way home. "However, transforming it from a hole into a door will take somewhat longer...

"We cut the hole, but then couldn't get the door to hang straight. We fitted it and refitted it about three times, but it was still not hanging properly. In the end, we've had to leave it and we'll work on it again tomorrow."

At least when I arrived on D-Day + 1 (Door Day + 1) we had a hinged closure with a five-point security lock that couldn't be lifted off its hinges protecting the truck's interior from thieves and the weather. Well, almost.

"How was your day?" revealed, "We struggled to get the door to fit flush, so there is a small gap, but I don't think it's too much of a problem."

It wasn't too much of a problem until we discovered months later that the door can't withstand driving rain from the wrong direction. In that uncommon conspiracy of precipitation and orientation, it acts like a doorman at The Ritz and admits only the more elite droplets. The ones not wearing trainers and a T-shirt. Unfortunately, such lackadaisical dress sense is rare among raindrops, so in wet weather, we have to be extremely mindful of which way we face.

Shortly before we left, Miles proudly showed off the day's accomplishments to me.

"See those oversized, rounded bolts on the frame. They were my idea. They set t'door off perfectly!"

Once again, the ghost of Miles past echoed in my head. *It'll look good for t'photos, but nowt will work.*

mRNA-Tastic!

As over-50s, Mark and I received our first coronavirus vaccination on 27th February. This was one thing Britain got right during the pandemic. When the vaccine became available, the best estimate for us to receive our shots had been the following November. To be protected nine months ahead of schedule, opening up the glorious possibility of a vaccination passport to allow us to travel once restrictions lifted, was a thrilling bonus.

Vaccination centres had sprung up all over the country: in Scout huts, church halls, and even gazebos in car parks.

A huge volunteer force made it run like clockwork. Meeting and greeting, noting down names, and observing patients for fifteen minutes post-jab to ensure they didn't grow a second green head, or experience all the other weird reactions publicised by the anti-vaccination campaigns.

Mark couldn't comprehend my biochemist's delight at getting the Pfizer vaccine. I'd experienced the forefront of biotechnology. It was mRNA-Tastic!

I had absolutely no side effects and came out as completely normal as before...

A Girl's Best Friend

According to one of Mark's managers, "You and Jackie aren't just a married couple. You're best mates!"

For my 57th birthday, my bestie bought me a fine selection of thoughtful gifts.

Six sand ladders to help us escape when bogged down in sand or mud. A 22-tonne bottle jack, should we need to change a wheel. Two heavy-duty shackles to attach tow ropes to the truck, plus a pair of soft shackles as a safe way to join my new matching pair of kinetic recovery ropes, which were as thick as my wrist. (Soft shackles are made of rope, so if they snap under tension, they don't catapult chunks of metal shrapnel through the air.)

Mark's smorgasbord of gifts thrilled me.

In an overland rescue situation, diamonds aren't a girl's best friend.

Give me a kinetic recovery rope any day!

Water Water Everywhere – But Not A Drop to Drink

The Beast's fresh water tank posed more conundra than the door.

First, where to get it?

Then, where to put it?

Mark wanted a square tank, but couldn't source one anywhere. All the drinking water tanks we found were cylindrical; an awkward shape to fit into a rectangular truck.

Miles helpfully crammed all our message channels with images and links to cubist water tanks. "There's LOADS available!" he berated us.

Indeed, there were, but they were not *potable* water tanks.

Potable water tanks store water that is safe for human consumption. Their construction adheres to strict standards and often incorporates a specialised coating or liner.

If all you want to do is irrigate your garden in a drought, you can live with a few toxic chemicals leaching out of the plastic into your H_2O, but I didn't fancy making them into tea.

When it came to location, Miles pointed out,

"There's loads of room under the chassis. It's only nine bolts. If we drop the prop shaft, we could fit it under there."

Literally, until I wrote that sentence, I believed Miles wanted to relocate the prop shaft permanently to accommodate the water tank. In my ignorance, I was immovable on the matter. I was dead against the idea of making such a major mechanical modification to the truck.

Mark has since explained that Miles meant unhitching the prop shaft, fitting in the tank, then fixing the running gear back in its rightful place.

However, even though he understood Miles's intentions more clearly, he wasn't keen on fiddling around with such a critical component, either.

Eventually, we sourced a rectangular 350-litre potable water tank, which would fit neatly in the space between the cab and the truck body, next to the spare wheel.

Then, all we had to do was find a new welder to make a frame to support it.

Thankfully, Tez and his oxy-acetylene cylinder rode in to save the day.

He set to work on the steps and rear bike platform/storage box, as well as constructing a receiver to hold the water tank.

Unfortunately, we had all missed one crucial detail.

Insulation.

Our plans for The Beast were as both a ski bus and a carefree summer retreat.

In a Continental summer, tepid tap water might not be the most refreshing beverage, but in sub-zero Alpine temperatures, an uninsulated water tank would be an ice machine second to none.

Tez was precise in his measurements.

He made the frame exactly the right size for the tank.

With no margin to add insulation.

Coronavirus Update

On Monday 22nd February, the UK government announced its long awaited roadmap out of lockdown. After almost 50 days of stay-at-home regulations, this was more than welcome.

It was a four-stage plan, 'based on data, not dates', which depended on certain conditions, being met, such as vaccination rates.

The earliest date proposed for all restrictions to be lifted in England was 21st June.

Chapter 17
March 2021

365 Days Into The Build
Overrun – 5 Months
Time to Third Completion Deadline – 2 Months

Buying the Worktop

One evening in March, Mark got a message from Miles.

"Get here early tomorrow and we can go over to my mate's at Verwood to buy a piece of wood for the worktop."

For six months, we'd had four filthy, grey cobwebby planks propped up behind the television in our lounge. When they arrived, I'd asked Mark what they were.

"That's our kitchen worktop," he announced proudly. "We need to keep them indoors to dry them out."

He must have noted my expression. With almost messianic fervour, he explained the miracle that lay before me, masked by mildew. I was an unbeliever! All it would take to reveal the inner beauty of the seasoned wood was a good sanding and a coat of varnish.

During the coronavirus lockdown, we'd watched quite a lot of daytime TV. By the end of Mark's sermon, I was almost confident that tying the planks together with bow-shaped butterfly joints, as we'd seen on some upcycling programme like *Repair Shop/Money for Nothing/Find It, Fix It, Flog It*, would look rather artisan.

But I still had some reservations.

The only thing greater than my dislike of louvre doors and other domestic dust traps is my aversion to chips, gaps, or cracks in crockery or food preparation areas. I am a biochemist, so I understand precisely what microbial horrors lurk in the scratches and scores on a chopping board.

A worktop composed of formerly filthy conjoined planks sounded like a pathological nightmare to me. But with tempers frayed and stress levels running high on the build, I'd learned to choose my battles carefully.

The prospect of an unsullied, solid wood worktop coming out of nowhere was godsent.

I've mentioned how the simple question, "How was your day?" could lead to a humorous yarn. A giggle over dinner. Or a droll re-counting of some amusing episode over a glass of wine.

Or, it could act as the blowtorch to the blue touch paper of Kraka-toan explosion, followed by hours of "I don't believe it"s and "What the f@*!"s.

On the occasion of Mark and Miles going to choose the worktop, "How was your day?" definitely yielded one of the most memorable responses.

I will pass you over to Mark for a first-hand recollection of the day's events.

When I arrived at 10 a.m., Miles said, "Give Iain a ring. He might want to come along for the ride and a change of scenery."

I called, and Iain replied, "I was just about to eat."

"I can get you a burger later," I said.

"I need something now. Have I got time to do some food?"

"No. We're leaving immediately, so we'll be with you in five minutes. I'll buy you something at the shop."

"Have I got time to make an omelette?"

"Not really! I'll stop at the shop and we'll grab a burger later."

"I need something healthy."

"Iain, it's your choice. Do you want to come with us or not?"

He thought for a second, then said, "I'll come."

As I hung up, Miles asked,

"What was all that about?"

"Iain wanted something to eat. He wanted to make an omelette."

Miles grimaced. "He's going to be a pain," he replied. "Tell him not to come."

"It's already arranged and it'll be fine. We'll go via the shop and get him a sandwich. Give me the address of the wood place, and I'll put it into Big Blue's satnav."

"I've got it on my phone. Let's just go."

"Miles, it's much easier if the satnav directs me and you don't have to tell me every turn. What's the postcode?"

"I don't have a postcode. Only the address."

I plugged in the address, and we set off: to collect Iain, take Iain to the shop, then endure mild bickering between the pair of them until the satnav said we were within two miles of the destination. Which turned out to be in Fordingbridge, not Verwood.

Then Miles suddenly shouted, "Turn left here!"

"But the satnav says straight on," I replied.

"TURN LEFT HERE!" he yelled.

I turned left and got to another junction, where Iain piped up,

"It's right here."

"No, it's not," said Miles. "Do you even know where we're going?"

"No, but I know this area really well."

"Do you know Bill?" Miles asked.

"No..."

"Then how do you know where he lives? You don't know where we're going. MARK. GO LEFT!"

After driving for two miles, I gently mentioned that we were moving further from the destination, not closer. The satnav indicated we were now four miles away, not two.

But Miles disagreed.

"Four miles? My phone says it's only half a mile."

After a further two miles of searching, we were none the wiser, but we were getting warmer. Once again, the satnav determined we were two miles away. Miles still insisted we searched that area, even though the address was elsewhere. He told me,

"Bill's got a workshop at his dad's house. I'll recognise the lane when I see it."

Miles and Iain continued bickering about which way to go.

"I know this area," Iain kept saying.

"But you don't know where we're going!" Miles yelled back.

I just stayed out of it.

Then Miles said, "Stop at the Co-op and I'll ask. They're bound to know in there."

We stopped, and they knew, although later, it transpired that they didn't.

When he came out of the shop, Miles was jubilant. "It's at the garage over the roundabout. I know where it is!"

We drove past the point where the satnav had directed us.

We drove past the spot where, an hour ago, we initially deviated from where the satnav directed us.

Then we reached the garage.

"There it is!" Miles said. "There's a sign for his business."

"There is a wood supplier here, where the Co-op sent us," Iain confirmed.

Miles looked more closely, then said, "It's not him."

"It sounds similar, though," Iain added.

"I'll go and look," Miles said.

Big Blue hadn't even stopped rolling before Miles exited stage left.

He came back a few minutes later and said, "It's not here, but they told me where he is."

I put in a new postcode and we headed back whence we came.

It took us to a skip hire business in the middle of nowhere.

We asked there, and they directed us back to the garage.

"No, that's a different company," Miles argued with the skip hire people. "We've already been there. He's around here somewhere."

The skip hire man said, "I've been here fifty years. That's the only wood yard I'm aware of."

Undeterred, Miles instructed me to carry on driving on the basis, "I'll recognise it when I see it."

"Have you called him?" Iain asked.

"Yes! Twice on his mobile and twice on his landline, but there was no reply. And he didn't respond to any of my messages."

"When did you see him last?" Iain continued his interrogation.

"I got some wood from him about four years ago. He'll have what we need."

"Have you told him we're coming?"

"No. I haven't spoken to him."

"Has he put something aside for us?"

"No, but he'll have something to suit."

Mentally, I slapped my forehead, but kept quiet. I didn't want to cause any more conflict.

We drove up and down a few more lanes, but Miles saw nothing he recognised.

By then, I'd had enough. Going up one road, back down another, with the two of them squabbling like schoolkids.

"We need to head back," I told them. "This is pointless. We're just going round in circles."

"WAIT!" Miles said. "I'll call John. He'll know where it is."

I've no idea who John is, but after multiple calls, lost signals, and redials, we had directions.

We found a road John had named – which was the first positive sign all day.

"Okay," Miles said. "There'll be three roads on the right with a signpost. We need the third one."

We passed a road with a sign, but it was on the left. After that, we saw no other signposts.

Since we'd been on the right track with the first road, I said,

"Why don't we call John back?" but Miles said,

"No! He's working. I can't disturb him again. TURN RIGHT HERE!"

We turned right into a private estate. For the second time, Miles leapt out of the moving vehicle to collar two men working in a garden.

They had no idea where Bob's place was, so finally, we bailed out and went home.

By that time, we'd completely wasted five hours.

We'd failed to get a non-existent piece of wood, from a person we hadn't contacted, from a company Miles hadn't visited for four years, at a postcode we didn't have, in an 'easily recognisable road' that he couldn't recognise, that was in Fordingbridge, not Verwood.

Then Miles said, "He must have moved."

And that was my day!

A whole day lost because Miles refused to phone ahead or even confirm where the place was before we left because he was adamant he'd recognise it when he saw it.

At least Miles had the good grace not to charge us a day's labour, but all that wasn't the best of it.

Mark's shoulders started shaking.

While we were driving home, Miles said,

"Fancy making it so hard for people to buy something. How can anyone run a business like that?"

Mekkin' A Feature out of a F@*! Up

By now, Miles had constructed the framework for the bed and built the arms of the sofa around our two twelve-foot-long SUPs (Stand Up Paddleboards). They slid in on their edges from the rear doors.

When I collected Mark at the yard that day, Miles asked him,

"Have you shown her t'volcano and t'brick?"

When Mark admitted he hadn't, Miles produced two chunks of shaped, stained, and varnished wood. The first was brick coloured and brick sized, with slightly wavy edges. The other was a similarly sized navy-blue pyramid.

Miles was matter-of-fact.

"We've med a feature out of a f@*! up," he said, by way of explanation.

"We shaped the sofa's arms around the nose of the SUPs to make more space for the seats down the side, but that didn't leave enough room underneath to fit the twelve-volt cigarette-lighter power outlets we wanted to put there. They're quite deep, so we'll mount t'volcano and t'brick on the arms and they can slot in there.

'Mekkin' a feature out of a f@*! Up' would become a bit of a catchphrase during our build!

Chapter 18
April 2021

393 Days Into The Build
Overrun – 6 Months
Time to Third Completion Deadline – 1 Month

Coronavirus Update

On the 12th of April, Step 2 of the government's COVID-19 Roadmap out of Lockdown came into force. The regulations still forbade socialising indoors, but the Rule of 6 permitted up to six people from two households to meet outside. Working from home was encouraged, although all shops opened, along with outdoor entertainment and campgrounds. The advice said that domestic travel was allowed, but should be minimised. Anyone travelling abroad without a legally permissible reason faced a £5,000 fine.

Windows Part 1

In April, after a 12-week wait, our custom-made, metal-framed, double-glazed security windows finally arrived. We had seven of them strewn around our lounge like a bubble-wrapped art installation. Two replaced the manky worktop planks behind our television. The rest leaned gracefully against walls, the dining table, or peeking out from the back of the sofa.

Mark made the mistake of gently trying to persuade Miles to install them the following Monday. The only positive: at least Monday wasn't April Fools' Day.

We all had reservations about fixing the windows using only glue and asked the lovely Victoria at Kellett's Windows for advice and reassurance. Victoria was an absolute pleasure to deal with. A conversation with her was always uplifting, even when it was as anxiety inducing as this one.

"Most of my customers apply the correct super strength Sikaflex and nothing else," she told us. "There's no need for screws or bolts, but it's imperative to get the bonding right first time. Really, it's a professional job, because once they're in – they're in, if you get my drift. You absolutely must know what you're doing and use the right adhesive with the appropriate cleaner and primer, because they improve the Sikaflex's bond."

We had sourced some Sikaflex292-i, Primer-206 G+P, and Sika Cleaner 205, but recalled Miles urging us to buy cheaper products from a builder's merchant.

"Those are less expensive," Mark argued, "but they aren't as strong as the marine structural adhesives."

Mindful of Miles' relaxed approach, Mark tried to emphasise in writing the most crucial details of the window installation.

I appreciate I'm being a bit paranoid about the windows because there are no fixings other than the glue, and I know you know how to do it, but there are a couple of specific comments that seem important. I have summarised the lengthy instructions as briefly as possible.

Mark listed the key points, which were quite finicky. *Do not clean with solvents. Use activator sparingly with moist (not wet) lint-free towel. Change the towel after each wipe. Do not apply excessively or it may lessen the bond.*

As well as many other factors critical to the success of the installation, it was imperative that the glue dried at a temperature of 10 or preferably 15°C (50-59°F).

Miles was not a detail man, so Mark hoped he'd take note. As Mark pointed out, *the implications are obviously serious if we get it less than perfect.*

Mark ended with:

Maybe we can cut out the two rear and the small bathroom windows on Monday and fit them on Tuesday while there's a break in the weather.

Miles replied by return, once again accusing Mark of having too much time on his hands. *Calm down,* he urged. *You're doing my head in with your constant emails. What's the point of cutting holes then not fitting the windows until the following day?*

Then he ordered Mark to stop filling his mind with stuff he didn't need in it, turn his laptop off *please,* and bring whatever he needed for Monday. We didn't even get the usual punch-pulling LOL as a sign off.

The days of, "This will be a breeze. You two are so relaxed about it," was a far distant memory.

Mark was indignant. He leapt to his own defence,

Last email, but in answer to your question, it gets the cutting done so we can install the windows first thing the following morning. That gives them a full day to dry at the correct temperature. If we cut and fit on the same day, it will be late when we do the fitting. The daytime temperature will have fallen, so the glue won't set. It makes sense to me.

I must defend myself and say that in the last week, we've only had email comms on three subjects.

> 1. *You sent me to purchase the shower tray, and I told you it was a five-week wait, so I asked you to order the rest of the shower in case we had similar delays with that.*

> 2. *Me wanting to pay you some money for your labour.*

> 3. *The windows, as I only spotted the weather forecast today and thought it worth grasping an opportunity for a weather-dependent job.*

Sorry if I'm stressing you, but we have had over a year to do this and now, it's a rush at the end, which is stressing me too. I'm usually very laid-back about such stuff, and I'm trying to be cool.

Mark and I were becoming increasingly frustrated at being stuck in one place, particularly now restrictions were lifting. Plus, each month's delay depleted our retirement fund by nearly £1,500 in rent and bills.

For our sanity and our bank balance, we needed to get back on the road.

The Worktop Part II

Finally, Miles remembered the location of his friend, Bill's, wood yard. He, Iain, and Mark set out again one sunny afternoon. This time, they returned with a beautiful slab of sequoia (giant redwood). More than half a metre deep and two metres long, the heartwood was the rich earthy red of a prize Hereford cow, bordered by a wavy edge of yellow-blond sapwood. Untreated, the colour, grain, and knots were already gorgeous. Sanded and oiled, it would look stunning.

Mark had also bought a smaller piece of spalted hornbeam. (Spalting is the decorative effect of fine black lines in wood, caused by a fungal infection.)

The section of hornbeam was extra special.

On seeing the hornbeam for sale, Mark told Bill, "There's a hornbeam tree in the gardens near our apartment. Apparently, it's the oldest maiden (unpollarded) hornbeam in the UK. The Earl of Malmesbury planted it in 1740 to celebrate King George IV's betrothal to Princess Caroline of Brunswick."

Bill knew it well.

His planks of spalted hornbeam came from that very tree!

Jim, our local woodsman, had removed a failing branch from the VIP hornbeam and sold it to Bill. That single bough weighed 26-tonnes.

When he showed it to me, Mark said, "I would have bought the hornbeam for our worktop, but it cost three times as much as the sequoia."

We thought back to Jim's offer to remove the branch and take it away for free. He had to factor in his time and the expense of a low loader, but at £750 for a single plank, he must have made a tidy profit!

Mark and I shared a contrite glance.

A few years before, our historic hornbeam had dropped another limb. A fellow resident had kindly sliced it up with his chainsaw. We'd giggled as we sat in front of our open fire, warmed by red wine and a conflagration of 270-year-old logs.

Miles was neither giggling nor drinking red wine when he started work on the sequoia worktop, although alcohol of any kind would have undoubtedly been welcome.

"Bill must have kept this outside," he complained. "It's wet through and can you see here? Between the heartwood and sapwood? It's full of dry rot."

I felt the customary sinking feeling that had accompanied almost every element of the project, but Mark set to work to save the day.

He spent hours digging out the dry rot with a chisel. Then, he sanded and smoothed the worktop. We bought some ocean blue resin to make a 'river table', by filling in the channels left by the rot. But once sanded, the grooves showed off the wood grain beautifully. The meandering depressions not only complemented the undulating contour of the worktop's front edge, but had a practical application in catching crumbs and spills.

So, we left it as it was.

In the end, our worktop was no rectangular hunk of lumber. It was a sinuous, organic masterpiece, crafted by nature.

When he saw it, Miles enthused, "That's brilliant! Another feature out of a f@*! up!"

Yet, as Miles drilled holes for the various fixings and cut the apertures for the sink and hob, liquid water poured out of the timber. I'd just read a book about a couple who renovated a French country house. Their carpenter fitted a huge lump of wood as a mantlepiece.

Because it was unseasoned, it shrank and warped as it dried out.

My anxiety levels hit the stratosphere.

Unlike the grotty planks that had spent months exchanging moisture with the air behind the television in our lounge, we had no time to dry out the worktop if we wanted to complete our build on schedule.

Miles knew wood.

He was a talented carpenter.

We just had to trust that at some unspecified point in the future, the wood would not curl back from our hob and sink like the lips of a snarling wolf, and cause them to slip down into the cupboards below.

Windows Part II

Finally, when it stopped raining and warmed up, Miles and Mark got around to installing the windows.

When I turned up to admire them, Miles collared me and ranted,

"He's filled it from the inside! Everyone knows you don't fill from the inside. Rain will get in between the insulation and t'skin!"

On the ride home, I didn't have to ask, "How was your day?" to spark the tirade. Like a well-shaken soda bottle on the passenger seat, a quietly fuming Mark erupted.

"Measure twice. Cut once!" he yelled. I winced with each emphasis.

"I measured all the windows accurately. I double-checked the measurements, then I checked again. I left Miles to make the holes. The first two windows slid in like gloves. Absolutely perfect. But when we fitted the third one, on the far side of the truck, there was a massive gap between the window frame and the truck body. Miles accused me of drawing the lines in the wrong place, so I went and got the chunk of metal he'd removed. He'd cut it miles away from the line I drew! When we did that one, it was getting late and he was getting bored. He cut it from the inside because he couldn't be bothered to move the platform around to the other side.

"It rained last night. When I got there this morning, water was p***ing in through the gap. I had to do something. I know you shouldn't, but I shoved in loads of filler from both sides. At least I'm positive it's watertight."

As with the sink and hob in our unseasoned worktop, the slightly wonky fitting of the door, and so many other aspects of our build…

Time would tell.

Nomadland

The pandemic delayed the 93rd Academy Awards ceremony by two months. When it eventually took place on the 27th April, the film, *Nomadland*, won three Oscars: for Best Picture, Best Director (Chloé Zhao) and Best Actress (Frances McDormand).

The movie is based on true stories documented in Jessica Bruder's book, *Nomadland: Surviving America in the Twenty-First Century*. It follows Fern, recently widowed and laid off from her job, who was forced to move into a van to seek work. While travelling, she meets others who have fallen on hard times through divorce, healthcare bills, or losing their jobs and homes in the aftermath of the 2008 recession. To manage financially, they became modern day nomads, living in vans, caravans, RVs, or buses.

A review of the film on a blog I follow commented that there was no such equivalent of aged nomadic van-dwellers in Europe. They said all the full-timers they had met embraced the lifestyle.

I begged to differ.

In the same way as the bloggers, Mark and I achieved financial independence by saving hard, then renting out our property. We chose to travel, although we had to figure out how to survive without jobs when burnout and redundancy left us too ill to work. Still, nobody could argue that being forced into realising your long-held dream was all bad.

When we toured in our caravan at home and abroad, we frequently met middle-class early-retirees like ourselves. No one was there through necessity: it was purely for fun.

But, have you ever noticed how the people you meet or hang out with share a similar background or outlook to yourself? Perhaps even the same ethnicity?

You've heard the saying, 'Birds of a feather flock together'. Obviously, if you have common interests, you will come across like-minded souls. But this is also an example of the 'Similar-To-Me' effect, a form of cognitive bias.

Cognitive bias is a sneaky puppet master in our minds, which causes us to favour ideas, people, or beliefs that align with our own. Subconsciously, it makes individuals choose friends who share values, ideologies, and experiences. It locks us in a reverberation chamber where we all reinforce our shared biases because they reflect straight back at us, only louder and more convincingly, because everyone we know thinks the same.

Add in social media, and your cognitive bias gets worse.

Algorithms analyse our likes, clicks, and shares. Like an unadventurous chef, they continually dish up an online buffet they are confident we will devour, because it's chock full of our favourite comfort food.

Algorithms don't ask us to sample challenging flavours.

They keep us on safe ground. Cocooned from diversity. Enveloped in cosy familiarity.

Cancel culture swiftly kicks in for those who dare step out of line. We have the power of the delete button. We can erase comments, block dissenting views, or unfriend – and thus preserve the status quo of our unshakeable certainty.

While working on the truck with Miles, Mark and I were lucky enough to meet an entire community of people we didn't know existed.

Most were content with their lifestyle.

Many, like Miles, were self-employed. Artisans who sold their wares online or at festivals. Digital creators, free to work from any location with an internet connection. Or tradespeople who flitted from project to project all over the country. However, there were also some who had fallen through the cracks because of mental health issues, unemployment, or broken relationships.

Britain is justly proud of its Welfare State. A financial, social, and healthcare safety net designed to support all citizens 'from the cradle to the grave'.

The problem is that if you tumble from the edge of society's grid, it's almost impossible to clamber back on.

With no fixed address, you don't exist. You can't get a job, benefits, or access services, loans, or credit – all of which rather scuppers your chances of getting that vital fixed address.

But it can happen to anyone. A fellow van lifer, Kate, told me the saddest tale of a chap she'd met begging on the streets, holding a sign saying, "Don't Judge." His story was tragic. He wasn't lazy, or on drugs. He'd owned his own successful one-man business, but his wife died suddenly, then he lost his daughter in an accident. Stricken with grief, he became too poorly to work. From experience, I can tell you that Statutory Sick Pay is barely enough to keep you in baked beans, never mind cover your bills and maintain a roof over your head. His mortgage payments slipped into arrears, so he lost his house. A childless single man is not a priority on the long waiting lists for social housing. Without an address – well, we just discussed that.

With businesses struggling to weather Brexit and the pandemic, it worried me that stories like this would become more common. Yet, the government was determined to enact its Police, Crime, and Sentencing bill, which would criminalise those who choose – or are forced – into an alternative lifestyle.

It's not all bad news, though.

Cliffe, the guy who said he never took food for granted and lived in a car with his dog, inspired me when he declared, "I'm a king, because I'm free!"

Yet, in the UK in the twenty-first century, in one small town in the prosperous south of England, we've met at least thirty households who live in vehicles full time.

In Britain, the world's sixth largest economy by GDP (Gross Domestic Product), I can assure you.

Nomadland is alive and well.

The Interior

Suddenly, the interior build started coming together. The worktop was in. The hob and sink hadn't dropped through it. And finally, Miles messaged me to say,

"Fridge fitted and running. Tell Mr. L he can relax. LOL!"

That was certainly a relief.

Not just getting a good-natured LOL to sign off. The world's priciest fridge had been with us so long, its guarantee was due to expire!

Miles had lots of things lying about his yard. Something he really loved was a vintage Wave Graffiti surfboard. White with blue rails, and the odd radical flourish of 1990s fluoro colours which made its hand-drawn graphics pop.

"Look at that. It's beautiful. Wave Graffiti created rideable art!" he said.

Ever the innovator, Miles sliced off the nose and fixed it upright to the end of our worktop. I adored how it formed a quirky and colourful divider to separate the kitchen area from the lounge while reflecting our passion for the ocean. The surfboard's tail, with its triple fin assembly, had the potential to be repurposed into a unique and stylish coat rack. Unfortunately, we had to forgo that idea because the fins were quite sharp and jutted out so far, we couldn't find anywhere to mount it safely.

Yet, despite the leap in progress, it was clear we weren't on course to complete the build by the 1st of May.

We pushed back our deadline.

Miles was so confident that The Beast would be finished, we gave notice to our landlords.

On the 30th June, if the truck wasn't ready, we would be homeless.

Chapter 19

May 2021

423 Days Into The Build
Overrun – 7 Months
Time to Fourth Completion Deadline – 2 Months
Time Until Homeless – 8 Weeks

Coronavirus Update

O n May 10th, for the first time since the previous July, no COVID-19-related deaths were reported in England, Scotland, and Northern Ireland. From 17th May, Step 3 of the Roadmap Out of Lockdown came into force, with further easing of restrictions. Groups of up to 30 people could meet outdoors. Indoors, the rule of 6 applied, but pubs, restaurants, accommodation, leisure facilities, and events were all open for business. Domestic travel was unrestricted, and the government now permitted overseas trips to 'green list' countries, where infection rates were low.

The EU announced it would allow fully vaccinated UK holidaymakers to visit, but by the 26th, France imposed mandatory quarantine on British tourists, due to the spread of the highly contagious COVID-19 variant first identified in India.

The Shower

"Orange or tequila sunrise?" Miles hollered.

"What?" I replied.

I'd dropped Mark off and was driving out of the yard when Miles materialised at Big Blue's window like a mysterious genie.

"For t'shower cubicle."

"I can't decide just like that on something I have to live with *forever*. My friend Helen's waiting and I'm late. I'll have a think and give you a ring."

The shower had gone through several iterations. In the end, rather than settling for ready-made-and-featureless in white, wipe-clean plastic, we opted for another adventure. We'd build the cubicle ourselves.

I know.

Our taste for trouble rivalled that of a cat with an unwavering affinity for cuddling up to cacti.

Miles had already warned us about the horrors of thin, acrylic shower trays.

"They crack in no time," he said, so we commissioned one to be fabricated in stainless steel. Besides its rugged industrial chic, which would rather suit The Beast, stainless steel would last forever.

From the café, after deliberating the shower cubicle conundrum with Helen, I called Miles to deliver my verdict.

"Tequila sunrise," I decreed.

I could tell he approved of my decision.

Deep orange at floor level, fading to a paler shade of ochre at the top.

"It's what I would have gone for," he enthused.

His ultimate plan was to construct the cubicle from burned and stained spruce ply to tie in with the rest of the interior. To make it watertight, he'd line it with clear PVC sheets.

It seemed simple enough.

I don't know what made me think an experimental shower cubicle would be anything but straightforward.

Rob the Roadie

One of the most inspiring people we met at a goat curry night was Rob the Roadie. A skilled electrician and engineer, he had worked backstage for some of the biggest names in the music business.

Our affection and admiration for Rob grew exponentially the more we got to know him, and he became instrumental in our build.

Mark and I love a Viking saga. That's how we developed The Shield Wall Analogy. A fine way to judge our relationships.

A shield wall was a formidable Viking battle formation. Soldiers stood shoulder to shoulder, then interlocked their shields to form an impenetrable barrier.

The shield wall was a collective defence. Each warrior used their shield to cover not only themselves, but their adjacent comrade. In a shield wall, everyone depended on the guy next door for protection.

In the corporate world, we frequently encountered people who lacked the courage even to stand firmly in line. At the first sign of trouble, they'd scarper. Others would slyly open their defence to allow an enemy blade to strike you, then close ranks again and deny it was their fault. And we've all met those who would stand alongside and maintain they were on your side, while they discreetly slipped a dagger in between your ribs.

Rob wasn't the type of friend to stand firm next to you in a shield wall. Despite his understated appearance, he was a berserker. That special kind of warrior who would forsake the safety of the battle line to fight with reckless abandon out front. There, he would unflinchingly protect his fellows and strike fear into the hearts of the enemy. With that kind of loyalty on your side, life is blessed.

Rob's story was a wholly British version of *Into the Wild*.

John Krakauer's famous book tells the extraordinary true tale of Chris McCandless, a young man who finished college, but couldn't face the pre-determined path that was mapped out for his life. Driven by a desire for adventure and a rejection of social norms, he donated all his savings to charity, abandoned his possessions, and embarked on an extraordinary solo journey into the Alaskan wilderness to live off the land.

Rob told us, "After my apprenticeship, I got a job where my dad worked. On my first day, one of his mates said to me, 'That's it now for the next 50 years!'

"I walked out straight away.

"With a tent and whatever else I could fit on the back of my bicycle, I rode out to the New Forest and lived there for years.

"In the summer, I earned money working at festivals or as road crew for bands on tour. In the winter, I foraged and ate road kill."

Rob's lifestyle worked well until disaster struck.

"We were dismantling a set. It was nearly done, so I told everyone to knock off, and said I'd join them for a drink once I'd finished up. Trouble was, I slipped and fell from the stage. I broke my back and was out of action for months. The insurance refused to cover it, because

I shouldn't have been working alone. It doesn't always pay to do favours!"

At least the company who employed Rob had some sympathy for his predicament. They allowed him to live in a caravan behind their unit on an industrial estate. He kept an eye on things and paid them back when a group of ne'er-do-wells broke in, intending to rob the place.

"I chased them down the road," Rob said. "They came back the following day to apologise!"

I tried to imagine being pursued by Rob, with his eyes fixed on you like a rattlesnake ready to strike.

Unlike Iain, who called in favours from anyone and everyone, Rob was ferociously independent. He wouldn't accept help unless he'd earned it and refused point blank to claim any benefits. And unlike Iain, Rob would occasionally return our lunchtime favours by buying us breakfast or a bacon sandwich.

When we asked him how he coped in winter with less work, he replied, "I eat a lot of baked beans, rest in bed, and try not to expend too much energy."

Rob's engineering expertise was invaluable, and he spent hours tinkering with the steps. Despite its simple and ingenious design, it took some effort to get the angles right to ensure the unit rolled in and out smoothly, without snagging on the truck's chassis.

Like Miles, Rob had a few favourite catchphrases.

Now and then, with a glint in his eye, he'd wind up Miles with, "You can't ask a carpenter to do an engineer's job..."

His most regular observation, though, which was perfectly apt for our build, was, "Someone hasn't thought this through..."

Fabricator Fandangles

Dealing with stainless steel fabricators was a crash course in frustration.

We dropped off diagrams, and the fabricator quoted us five weeks to make the shower tray and deflector bars for the cab roof. The deflector bars would push tree branches up to stop them snagging on our solar panels.

"It's a small job," they assured us. "We can fit it in."

Week after week, we chased up our order.

To ensure they'd answer the phone, we soon learned to call from numbers they didn't recognise, although even this wasn't always successful.

On the due date, Mark and I made the ninety-minute round trip to Wareham. When we arrived, the fabricator was brief and unapologetic.

"Sorry mate. Lost your drawings."

I'm not quite sure what brand of magic Mark worked, but he may have pointed out politely that he'd driven a long way on their appointed collection date, and extolled the magic of modern telecommunications, which have replaced the lost art of telepathy, and could have achieved so much in pursuit of acquiring replacement drawings, informing us that our order wasn't, in fact, ready as promised, thus sparing us the ordeal of a wasted road trip.

Mark supplied replacement drawings. Ever one to take his own advice, he phoned several times to check on progress, but they'd got wise to our covert calling tactics. Whatever number we called from, they never answered, so we embarked on a second pilgrimage to Wareham.

This time, we got a casual, "Sorry mate. We forgot about it. Now you're at the back of the queue!" When pressed, they also confessed, "And we've lost the drawings again."

Mark might have been more persuasive in pointing out that they should have delivered weeks ago and questioned the fairness of being passed over once again through no fault of our own. Nay, through their actual incompetence.

Magically, the elusive drawings resurfaced.

Within a week, Mark and I took a third trip to Wareham and returned triumphant with our spoils. One hard-won set of deflector bars and a made-to-measure stainless-steel shower tray.

Toilet Training

In the illustrious world of van life, there is an old saying:

"Where two or three are gathered together, they shall be discussing toilets."

In nomadic circles, if you want to kick off a conversation with a stranger, "What do you do with your poo?" is almost the ice breaker of choice.

Caravan Kismet boasted a built-in chemical loo, but that wasn't an option for The Beast. Our particular poo predicament was the height of the truck. A permanently plumbed fixture would make a black waste tank a lofty challenge to access and empty.

Enter the compost loo. Darling of the eco-conscious, off-grid adventurer.

Our research uncovered some upsides. They use no water, so they require no plumbing. In theory, your waste isn't wasted – it turns into black gold! Something useful, eco-friendly, and easy to dispose.

Except that in a vehicle without a huge storage tank, even with a urine diverter (which also helps prevent the pong) your loo will fill before the composting is complete. If you've nowhere to nurture it for the year or so it requires to 'mature', it will just have to go in the bin.

This sounds uncomfortable, but it's okay.

In the UK, landfill is where 3-billion non-biodegradable, plastic, polymer gel, elastic, and poo-filled disposable nappies end up each year. (Worldwide, it's 167-bill!)

The scatological output of Britain's near 20-million cats and dogs is a few thousand tonnes per day. If the dog owners pick up, that goes to landfill in bags – some of which might even be eco-friendly and biodegradable. Soiled kitty litter goes the same way. If it's the silica gel type, though, that certainly won't decompose.

According to government statistics, in 2021, British water companies pumped raw sewage into rivers and the sea 375,533 times, over 2.7-million hours. Sometimes, it's legal – if heavy rainfall overwhelms the system. Other times, it's because fines cost less than sewage treatment, which safeguards profits, dividends, and the directors' six-figure bonuses.

Perhaps "What do you do with your poo?" should become a more popular question in mainstream society.

Far from flush and forget, Dame Vera Lynn's song *We'll Meet Again* could be the anthem for traditional methods of sewage disposal. Particularly if you're into wild swimming or watersports.

Done properly, desiccating waste in a composting toilet helps remove pathogens. So, even if it's not fully composted, you're already ahead of the sewage disposal curve – with an environmental gold star if you use biodegradable bags.

But a compost toilet is a complex creature.

To work effectively, they need the correct combination of moisture, oxygen, and temperature.

Some systems need power to stir and aerate the compost, or to run a fan which will eliminate odours. Plus, you need to carry a supply of composting materials, such as sawdust, moss, or coconut coir, which dries out the waste and helps stay the smell.

Composting loos are more expensive to buy, but the final nail in the composting coffin was size. To contain motors, fans, and a sizeable waste tank, they are often larger than your conventional camping convenience.

Size matters – especially when you intend to cram the can into your shower cubicle to save space.

After much debate, we decided on something simple and self-contained, which also saved the truck an additional aperture.

With all her windows, doors, and extractor fans, The Beast's pierced and punctured body already looked as though we'd catapulted her through an asteroid field.

So, we settled on a Porta Potti as our convenience of choice.

A portable loo with a chemical cassette may not be the stuff of sanitary dreams, but it was compact, practical, and easy on the wallet.

As Hoover is to vacuum cleaners, and Google to those who search, Porta Potti is the potentate of privies.

The transportable throne that reigns supreme.

The Shower Part II

Back at the yard, after coffee with Helen and issuing my tequila sunrise edict, all was not well.

Miles had built the shower in the front right-hand corner, but the PVC sheets wouldn't fit through the cubicle door. It was too low.

It was also too narrow to facilitate the passage of our brand-new Porta Potti.

Rob was outside, grinning and sucking on a roll up. I could almost hear his distinctive laugh as he mumbled his catch phrase under his breath.

"Heh, heh, heh. Someone hasn't thought this through!"

I left the boys fencing with jigsaws amid a cloud of expletives and escaped to the beach with the dogs.

When I got back, I admired my new tequila sunrise shower, albeit through a suffocating aura of male smugness.

"We made the door taller to get the PVC in, and when you disconnect the two halves of the Porta Potti for emptying, it fits through no problem," Mark said.

The PVC sheets effectively glazed the stained wood and really brought out its beauty. Fairy lights behind the roof panel glittered off vibrant chrome fittings and a water-saving aerator shower head.

But the innovation didn't stop there.

The lads ignored my appreciative murmurings as their focus suddenly shifted to the extractor fan.

Wired up in reverse, it didn't suck; it blew.

Iain leapt to his own defence.

He went full Bart Simpson.

"I didn't fit it. I wasn't even here that day. And I have the video to prove it."

What a strange thing to say.

Quietly, I wondered if he meant the video of him fitting the fan!

Upholstery

While Mark went off to work at the coal face every day, I gallantly tackled all the unimportant stuff, such as walking the dogs and making sure we had food on the table.

However, he did delegate one truck-related job to me, albeit a rather 'pink' task. He wanted me to sort out the upholstery.

This single, seemingly straightforward project turned into an impossible minefield of cost, lead times, and Catch-22s.

I contacted so many suppliers, I had to start a spreadsheet.

"I have the measurements," I'd say. "Can you give me a ballpark price?"

"We really need to see it," they'd reply.

"That's not so easy because the truck is not insured to drive, the sofa isn't finished, and it's sitting in the south of England while you're Wales/the Midlands/Lancashire/the South West."

In the initial stages, there was also a COVID travel ban in place.

A few delivered reluctant estimates, based on the dimensions I gave and a medium-priced fabric.

They were all in the many thousands of pounds, with lead times in the manys of months.

It was time we didn't have.

I decided the most straightforward approach would be loose foam cushions with made-to-measure removable covers. We'd had similar in the caravan, although 'removable' was more aspiration than reality. The covers had zips, but also fixed buttons that pierced through the foam, making removal a pipe dream.

This was a problem.

We are puppy parents to four puddle-diving hounds and are sometimes irresponsible with glasses of red wine.

The caravan's non-removable covers were white.

Light and bright they may have been, but they had to be masked at all times with dark, impermeable throws.

Since I had the luxury of designing The Beast from the ground up, I wanted something durable and stain-resistant, washable, and in what you might call a 'forgiving' colour. i.e. one that would disguise both our drinking habits and the pups' swamp obsession.

I learned so much about upholstery!

Do you know about the Martindale Rub Test? In the 19th century, Mr. Martindale had a brainwave. He dispatched an oscillating sandpaper disc up and down fabric to mimic wear. And here's the rub (I thank you!) – a rating of 25,000-30,000 rubs is good for heavy domestic use, while >30,000 is commercial quality.

Then there's Crib-5, or Ignition Source 5, which is a set of British safety regulations that specify fire resistance for commercial upholstery. Crib-5 treated fabrics are not flameproof, but resist ignition and reduce the spread of flames.

A good idea in a campervan with a gas hob.

I kept the postie busy with a barrage of fabric samples.

Most were brutally disappointing. Thin, fragile, unimaginative, and dull.

Then a swatch of Cristina Marrone washable, patterned chenille with a rub rating of 100,000 plopped onto my doormat.

The designs were Italian, so they were all fabulous, but one in particular captured my attention.

I adored it, but I had to sell it to Mark.

"It's too much!" he said when the vibrant orange, turquoise, and deep blue camouflage pattern from the Accento range seared his retinas.

"Those are the colours we already have in the truck, and it's a camo pattern with a twist. It fits in with The Beast's military origins."

"It looks more like The Beast got caught inside a rainbow factory during a bombing raid," he said. "The catalogue only shows that pattern as an accent against something plainer. None of the examples use it as the main fabric."

"'Be bold, and the forces of greatness will come to your aid,'" I said, misquoting Goethe, who I'm sure never had RV upholstery on his mind.

"Trust me. It will look amazing. And it certainly won't show any stains..."

***

Miles swooped in to the rescue on the upholstery front.

Through his extensive network of contacts, he put us in touch with Elena, a retired upholsterer who lived nearby. She still had her industrial sewing machine and enjoyed making cushion covers as a hobby. Her prices started at a very appealing £30.

A miniature bundle of energy, Elena was an absolute darling who leapt at the chance to visit The Beast to measure up. She noted down all the dimensions we needed to order foam for the cushions, then pointed me towards an online fabric calculator. This factored in matching up the pattern and worked out exactly how much material I needed to buy.

Elena quoted us a few hundred pounds to make up covers from our own fabric, with zips – and no fixed buttons – so they'd be fully removable.

I'd already tried to source foam-cut-to-size from a local company, but they told me they couldn't supply for weeks, and were so rude and awkward to deal with, I didn't feel they deserved the business, anyway. At least they gave me a good grounding for our dealings with fabricators.

Elena recommended a firm in Welwyn Garden City who would cut and ship foam to order.

"Don't forget the Deacon Wrap," was her parting shot.

"The what?"

"Deacon. Something like that. It fluffs up the cushions and makes them fill the covers nicely."

I looked up Deacon Wrap and discovered Dacron is a polyester fibre bonded to the foam to add loft. It's best covered with a silky stockinette outer, to stop it rubbing off and help the covers slide on and off more easily.

I placed an order for six pieces of Firm Luxury Reflex foam with a Dacron poly fibre wrap: 15 cm (5.9") thick for the seats, and 10 cm (3.9") for the backs.

They arrived within two days.

The fabric took a week, but when we dropped it all off with Elena, she promised us faithfully she'd have our covers ready for D-Day on the 30th of June.

Things were looking positive, but our world was about to unravel.

Miles was about to drop a bombshell of atomic proportions.

Chapter 20
June 2021

454 Days Into The Build
Overrun – 7 Months
Time to Fourth Completion Deadline – 1 Month
Time Until Homeless – 4 Weeks

Miles' Bombshell

A week later, with just under a month to go before we became homeless, Miles announced,

"My mate's got me a roofing job in East Anglia on £1,000 a week."

We were speechless.

He must have heard our jaws hit the floor. In his I'm-being-the-most-reasonable-person-in-the-world voice, he offered a simple justification.

"I can't turn down good money like that!"

Never one to overreact, I felt like screaming loudly into a hopeless void of despair before drowning myself in an ocean of anguish.

He'd had The Beast for fifteen months and his invoices, although refreshingly honest, showed he'd completed around six weeks' work.

Iain's Last Stand

461 Days Into The Build
Overrun – 7 Months & 1 Week
Time to Fourth Completion Deadline – 3 Weeks
Time Until Homeless – 21 Days

Relations between Miles and Iain were constantly uneasy, but just before Miles left for East Anglia, they had a terminal breakdown.

Iain had a hissy fit and stormed off the job for good. All because of a piece of string.

The next time I bumped into Caroline and Oscar, I had quite a tale to tell.

"How's it going with the truck?" she asked and settled down to enjoy the drama.

"Things have been better," I replied, with masterful understatement.

"Miles is leaving to start another job, and Iain's walked out. All because Miles wouldn't let him pull a wire through a conduit with a piece of string."

"What?"

"I know."

"But Iain's quit before and come back. Can't you persuade him again?"

"I don't think so. It got quite acrimonious. Miles lets Iain store some of his stuff in a lockup at the yard. When they fell out this time, Iain threatened to ruin Miles' business online. So Miles retaliated, and said he'd chuck all Iain's stuff in the river."

"Oh."

"I know.

"And Iain also accused Miles of turning us against him. Iain usually asks us to order wire and components in bulk. It's cheaper, but he likes to keep the surplus for himself. He pushes his luck occasionally. We know that, and Miles has picked him up on it once or twice. We don't mind. It makes him happy, so it's a win:win.

"The way Iain sees it, though, is that Miles has made the accusation to us that he has been systematically ripping us off. We assured him that wasn't the case, but whatever we say, he just won't believe us."

"So, you're in a bit of a fix."

"You could say that. We're three weeks from being homeless and don't have a complete interior, gas, or electrical system. Mark and Rob the Roadie will try to muddle through with finishing the essential bits of the build, but I don't know how anyone is going to pick up where Iain left off with the electrics. He's built it to a standard more appropriate to the Pentagon than an overland truck!"

"What are you going to do?"

I might have laughed hysterically.

The Final Showdown

The finale of Iain's cameo in our life was the day he came to collect the gear he'd stored in Miles' lockup.

Miles was away in East Anglia, as Iain well knew, but Mark and I were there with Rob, trying to race to the finish with the build.

Iain had roped in a friend with a van to transport his gear, and since he didn't have Miles' permission, he'd come with bolt cutters to remove the padlocks from the lockup.

Finally, Mark, whose dyke of discretion had been challenged by Miles' and Iain's foibles and outbursts for months, completely lost it.

His long-suffering levee of leniency fractured, and he detonated like Mount St. Helens, spewing molten tension and fiery rhetoric into the already volatile atmosphere.

"You are NOT destroying Miles' property," he yelled. "If you want your belongings, you arrange it with Miles."

The embarrassed-looking van driver cowered in the corner, while Rob stood back to admire the spectacle.

The driver, Swoop, one of our van life friends, looked sheepish and said, "He didn't say he didn't have permission."

I put my hand on Swoop's shoulder. "Don't worry," I said. "It's just Iain being Iain."

People underestimate Mark. His calm exterior belies the steely strength that lies beneath. Mark will do all he can to avoid conflict, but don't ever try to push him around.

After a lot more shouting, Iain realised he had reached an impasse.

Swoop escorted him away, and that's the last we ever saw or heard of him.

He departed with a brand-new electrical testing meter we'd bought on his instruction tucked under his arm. It was in a shiny blue and red box, unused and cellophane-wrapped. I could tell he didn't want to relinquish it, and I didn't have the heart to take it off him. That would have felt like stealing a new toy from a toddler on Christmas morning.

A few days later, Kate, who was working on her own conversion, shared her interactions with Iain, which very much mirrored our own,

"We've all driven to Poole to get him kerosene, taken him to the vape shop and Sainsbury's. I got him a bag of shopping and the next day, he was on the van life forum saying he was all on his own and no-one helps him!"

"You took him to Stonehenge for his friend's funeral, didn't you?" she said to us.

"Yes!" I replied. "And we gave him £100 of shopping to see him through Christmas, bought him lunch every day, carried jerry cans of water to save his bad back, invited him out for walks at the weekends so he wasn't alone in his van. He never thanked us once, and he hasn't offered us the video footage of our build that he took on the camera we gave him!"

Yet, although Iain let us down spectacularly, and left us with half an LPG installation, and a part-finished electrical system that would require someone with the aptitude of Nikola Tesla to decode, I don't resent any of the kindnesses we showed him.

He truly was a person in need. Deep down, he was genuinely kind and caring, in the same way that Miles truly wants to help people and was frequently very generous.

The problem was, they both had personality traits that acted like a blowtorch to ignite the other's blue touch paper.

Patience and understanding were not virtues either held.

And unfortunately, there was more of that to come.

Miles' Second Bombshell

465 Days Into The Build
Overrun – 7 Months, 2 Weeks & 4 Days
Time to Fourth Completion Deadline – 1 Week & 3 Days
Time Until Homeless – 10 Days

Miles's concession to dropping us in the *merde* was to break his own cardinal rule. Grudgingly, he agreed to drive back to The Vision Vault at weekends to complete work that Mark and Rob couldn't tackle alone.

Within a fortnight of starting, Miles had a huge bust up with his mate, and walked off the roofing job. Quietly, we heaved a sigh of relief. He hadn't turned down the money at our behest, and now he was free to come and finish the truck.

We couldn't have been more wrong.

He struck us dumb once again when he announced, "I'm going on holiday."

When our jaws hit the deck again with a force that probably registered on the Richter scale, in his best I-can't-believe-I-even-have-to-explain-this voice, Miles said,

"Look. I've been flat out on the truck for nearly eighteen months. For the last few weeks, I've been driving hundreds of miles back and forth, working seven days a week to finish *your* truck. I'm exhausted. I need to look after my mental health!"

As I stood next to Mark, I sensed an even greater eruption brewing. A supernova of missed deadlines and 'I'm not in today 'cos it's sunny/I'm taking the kids to the beach/I'm nicking the welder because there's a weather window and I need to work on my own van'. Almost a year of recriminations. Of Mark holding his tongue to keep Miles sweet, so he wouldn't quit and abandon us. It was all there, ready to push up like an earthquake, to boil over and explode like Old Faithful, and split the sky like the most epic lightning storm.

I placed my hand on Mark's arm.

Together, in silence, we walked to Big Blue and drove away from the yard.

***

Later, I sent Miles a message.

Miles, we're ten days from being homeless. Please can you not show some support in getting the truck finished? I understand you need to look after your mental health, but we need to look after ours.

Curiously, its understatement seemed to hit home.

By return, Miles messaged Mark

Can you call off your killer wife?

Something Rather Beautiful

454 Days Into The Build
Overrun – 7 Months, 3 Weeks & 5 Days
Time to Fourth Completion Deadline – 2 Days
Time Until Homeless – 48 Hours

With Mark and Rob working every day, and Miles joining in at weekends, we'd made some progress, but full completion was a big ask.

I uttered a phrase which, like 'Let's go to Mongolia,' would come back later to haunt me: "So long as we have water, gas, and electricity, it doesn't matter if we don't finish the cosmetic stuff."

But then, mere hours before we were homeless, something rather beautiful happened.

Unasked and unprompted, a whole community of van lifers mobilised and rallied to support us in our hour of need.

I drove into The Vision Vault to find Kate re-covering our cab head liner. Her partner Gerry was helping Miles with the woodwork. Rob was finishing the steps, roof bars, and packing insulation around the water tank. In between jobs or after work, Nicole's brother, Henry, a professional plumber, completed and certified the LPG gas installation. Alex, a qualified electrician, also dropped in when he could to make sense of our electrics. Along with his friend Darren, Alex ran regular self-build get-togethers, where everyone met up to socialise and help each other with their campervan conversions. He did what he could with Iain's electrical spaghetti, although inevitably, a few quirks remained. We had switches in all kinds of strange places – and the only way to turn off the fridge and water pump was to remove the fuses.

Amid this hive of activity, Mark was busy trying to cram our life into The Beast's ample rear, while I ferried our possessions from the apartment to the yard in Big Blue.

A couple of days earlier, Miles had used his best 'nothing-to-do-with-me!' voice to let me know, "You need to order some child locks to keep the kitchen drawers shut while you're driving."

I chose not to share my thoughts on how it might have been preferable to incorporate drawer closures into the design.

I searched online, but none of the options would work with our drawer configuration. At the last minute, Miles crafted me a solution. He cut a wooden batten to the right length to pass through the drawer handles. Then, he screwed a spring to the top so that I could wedge it underneath the worktop to keep it in place. It wasn't exactly what I'd had in mind, but it did the job!

He also gifted us a plasma-carved steel picture of a wolf that I'd admired, and one of his beautiful handcrafted mirrors, which he fitted next to our front door.

I first saw one of his surfboard-shaped mirrors in a windsurfing shop years before. I couldn't afford it, and had coveted one ever since. Now I had one, in his trademark tequila sunrise colours, to match our shower.

For the final time, we all gathered around the campfire to enjoy drinks, bonhomie, and a cook up.

Quietly, amid the hubbub, Rob said the loveliest thing to Mark.

"Watch where you go with that. The world's becoming a dangerous place. I don't want to have to come and get you out of a cell somewhere. You know I would, don't you?"

"I do." Mark clapped Rob on the shoulder. "That's why we're mates."

Chapter 21

1st July 2021

457 Days Into The Build
Overrun – 8 Months & 1 Day
Time After Fourth Completion Deadline – 24 Hours
Homeless

D-Day

On D-Day (Departure Day), our plan was to pack up and clean our apartment at leisure, then leave around midday for a slow meander to Alex and Darren's self-build campervan get together at Wantage, near Oxford.

The reasoning behind our initial stop was not only social. If anything went wrong with The Beast, we figured there would be someone there who knew which bit to clobber with a spanner. Plus, there was another lure. While fixing our electrics, Alex had let us into a secret,

"A TV crew from *Million Pound Motorhomes* is coming to film on the Friday. They're very interested in The Beast."

But at 20.30 on D-Day, we were still working flat out on the truck, fitting in the finishing touches between packing, cleaning, returning keys, and collecting The Beast's upholstery.

I recalled my foolish utterance: "So long as we have water, gas, and electricity, it doesn't matter if we don't finish the cosmetic stuff."

On D-Day, we had electric.

With his full time job, Henry couldn't come and sort out a few teething problems with the plumbing. Once again, the Ghost of Miles Past echoed in my head. *It'll look good for t'photos, but nowt will work.*

However, we had no option but to move into The Beast.

We were homeless.

A tenant was already moving into our apartment.

We had nowhere else to go.

Site rules forbade overnight stays at The Vision Vault. Tears pricked my eyes. It was late. Wantage was hours away. At a top speed of 45 mph, we had no chance of making our planned stop. We had no idea where to park our gigantic pantechnicon for the night.

Perhaps experiencing a twinge of compassion, Miles guided us to his secret wild camping spot in the New Forest. During our travels, he had also kindly agreed to host Big Blue as a guest at the yard, which would save hundreds of pounds in storage costs.

In a strange parallel with the day five years before, when we packed up our life to tour full time in Caravan Kismet, our maiden voyage started many hours late and was only a few miles.

For the very first time, I sat in The Beast's cab as she roared into life the second Mark turned the key. Miles filmed our departure as we rumbled out of the yard. We pulled over, so he could overtake and guide us slowly to his secluded park up.

We arrived as the sun dipped behind the horizon in streaks of mauve, apricot, and blue, reminiscent of the colours in our upholstery.

Utterly exhausted, we bade Miles goodnight, then cracked open a bottle of wine to toast this new chapter in our life.

In the field opposite, we watched a hobby, a rare bird of prey, hunt.

We designed The Beast to be fully functional off grid. She is much more versatile than Caravan Kismet, which needed the facilities of a campsite. Parked in an exquisite location, overlooking the rolling green countryside in the national park, things didn't seem so bad. Other than the water not working and a smell of gas under the hob.

We switched off the cylinder, and I kept the windows open. Just in case.

Well, we had electricity, and fortunately, I'd had the foresight to bring along several large bottles of emergency H_2O. We hung blankets over the windows, because the blinds we'd ordered hadn't arrived, and went to bed.

On the morning of D-Day-plus-one, Miles showed us how to locate a gas leak using dishwashing liquid.

"Put LOADS on. Where you see it bubbling, tighten the joint, 'cos there's your leak."

An immense military aircraft, a C17 Globemaster, overflew our park up several times. Either he was practising 'touch and gos' at Bournemouth airport, or it was a spy plane checking us out to make sure we weren't an invading force.

Our first morning also brought our first disapproving look.

A passing cyclist failed to appreciate the beauty that is The Beast. He turned up his nose when we proffered a friendly "Hi" as we walked The Fab Four around the layby.

It brought home that, despite our residence being the mansion house of motorhomes, we were now travelling folk. Officially on the wrong side of conventional society.

The divide between, "Oh WOW! Good for you. You're Living the Dream!" and "You're a worthless didicoy whom I automatically despise!" is slight.

Volvo Means 'I Roll'

Volvo is the first person conjugation of the Latin verb *volvere* (think 'revolve'). A Swedish ball bearing manufacturer selected it as a simple, memorable name that was easy to pronounce.

Volvo's logo, a circle with an arrow extending from the top right, represents masculinity, the Roman god Mars, and the alchemical symbol for iron. It was chosen to represent 'rolling strength'.

To my disgust, a few months previously, Mark had ventured,

"I don't think you'll be able to drive The Beast."

That was like a red rag to a bull.

"I can fly a frikkin' plane," I growled. "There's no reason I can't drive a truck!"

However, riding in the cab, I saw what Mark meant. Piloting The Beast certainly demanded some rolling strength.

With huge knobbly tyres and limited power assistance, steering was very physical, and gear changes required two feet of travel from the gear stick.

My role as passenger was equally interactive. Through the narrow lanes in a four-metre-tall, left hand-drive vehicle, my running commentary was worthy of a co-pilot in a rally car.

"Low-hanging branches right. Sharp left turn; fifty yards; clear. Road narrows ahead; bus approaching. Pedestrian left. Ten per cent gradient with hairpins. Oncoming cyclist..."

We stopped at Rownhams, the first service station on our route. Twenty miles in, we both felt drained. With no water or gas at this point, we really needed our first coffee of the day!

South Central Self-Build Meetup

At last, in the early evening, we rolled into the Self-Build meetup. We'd missed our shot at stardom with *Million Pound Motorhomes* by hours.

A two-point shuffle got us in through narrow stone gates and the cab rode through the canopies of an avenue of beech trees that lined the driveway. A welcoming committee filmed and photographed our spectacular entrance, so there was no pressure when Mark had to reverse The Beast around a corner on to our pitch through a second tight gateway, while avoiding an inopportunely placed pillar that interrupted our swing trajectory. He did it perfectly.

I high fived him. "Not bad, first time out."

Just as we switched off the engine, Nev, our neighbour whose large motorhome was blocked in behind us, came and asked,

"Can you move that, mate? I need to get out."

As with Miles, that's exactly the sort of inflammatory banter that kicks off a firm friendship.

Mark and I have many amazing talents, but as you now know, the technicalities of built-not-bought campervans don't number among them.

In truth, we were as green as our truck.

When Darren came to meet us, the conversation between him and Mark reminded me of the scene in the movie *Home Alone,* where Macaulay Culkin quizzes John Candy.

"What Make is she?"

"Volvo N10."

"How old?"

"30 Years."

"How big's the engine?"

"9.6 litres."

"V6 or V12?"

"Errr, not sure..."

"What configuration is the intermittent sprocket flange ball?"

"Um. Now, you've lost me..."

Awed crowds came to visit and asked where we intended to travel in such a magnificent vehicle. UK coronavirus restrictions were lifting, but the EU had banned British travellers. We had to admit that, because of COVID, our plans were now, "More Manchester than Mongolia".

But the UK is a beautiful country.

We looked forward to exploring all those places we had been saving for our frail dotage, when we'd be too old and jaded to overland across Kazakhstan.

No Regrets?

There is a saying, 'Shoot for the moon and even if you miss, you're still among the stars'.

It isn't true, of course.

For a start, the moon is 252,088 miles away while the distance to the nearest star, our sun, is 93 million miles. That's 368 times further! I won't mention the next one, Proxima Centauri. Okay, I will. It's 24,984,092,807,519 miles. So distant, it would take you 4.3 light years to get there. And light zips around at 186,000 miles per second, don't you know?

However, I like the sentiment.

Creating a home in the back end of a truck was always going to be a long and winding road, but despite all the hiccups, we were delighted with the result.

In a backlash against Caravan Kismet's tastefully inoffensive and neutrally unprovocative 'fifty shades of beige' interior, we'd gone for the 'explosion in a paint factory' look. Our aquamarine walls and ceiling, complemented by sunny coral and ochre cupboards in hand-stained wood, gave the decor our desired 'underwater' ambiance. I thought our 'tequila sunrise' shower cubicle and Italian camo sofa in retina-singeing hues of indigo, tangerine, and turquoise were a triumph. Perhaps it was lucky for The Fab Four that dogs are red-green colour blind.

At the get together, a steady stream of self-builders filed in to view our ample living quarters. It was easy to read the facial expressions of those who appreciated the kaleidoscopic exuberance, and those whose first reaction to the polychromatic pummelling was a jaw-flooring, "WTF?!"

Gradually, our services came on line.

By day two, following Miles and Alex's tender ministrations, we were cooking on gas and had cold running water.

By day six, three gas leaks and two water leaks into our travels, we managed a much-appreciated hot shower.

There is no doubt the project had tested our mettle.

In and of itself, it was a tough journey, but supporting others and living through COVID lockdowns had also been harsh.

At times, I'd felt so depressed I couldn't summon the enthusiasm to open a book or watch TV, let alone put pen to paper and write, my great passion. My relationship with Mark suffered. Unsurprisingly, unable to unleash his frustrations in the yard, he brought them home. My calm, laid-back man morphed into someone I barely recognised.

To remain 'the couple who didn't argue', I soon learned not to question anything. He often perceived my input as criticism. "Leave it to me. I'll sort it," became his stock phrase, even in areas where I had particular expertise – I'd worked for years as a product specialist in refrigeration and water filtration.

Yet, the excitement of owning The Beast always overrode the problems. We had never reached the stage of, "Let's just give up on the whole thing," and remarkably, Mark and I ended the build still together, and still friends with Miles.

Miles even helped us compile a list of his favourite catch phrases for the book he knew I'd write.

- "I'm surrounded by f@*!n' idiots!"

- "Bloody office workers!"

- "What's Laurel and Hardy up to now?" (referring to Mark and Iain.)

- "READ YER MESSAGES!"

- "BE COOL!" – when we worried about lead times and lapsing time frames.

When he asked, "What will you call the book?" and I replied, jokingly, "I thought about 'Truckin' Idiots'," I could tell he approved.

We knew that in opting to construct a completely unique camper from the ground up, we had not chosen a straightforward route. Nevertheless, the adventures she promised and our almost insane obsession with "There's always a solution!" saw us through.

Miles's stunning craftmanship makes The Beast a striking one-off. I even embrace her imperfections – they add character, and they're *our* quirks and flaws!

Certainly, Miles helped us bring in the project at a fraction of what it could otherwise have cost. Even taking into account the extra rent, bills, and subsequent retro-fits, our truck twin spent more than double on his professional conversion. Although when people ask "How much does a conversion like that cost?" I reply,

"Your soul . Possibly your sanity."

With a company shouldering the burden of design and execution, that is not an answer my truck twin will ever be able to give. While these projects never go completely to plan, the basis of his tale is much simpler than ours. 'Bought the truck. Handed it over. Got it back complete.'

Which is why he still has all his hair and hasn't gone grey.

Would we do it again?

DEFINITELY!

Now we know what it involves, and have the network of contacts, we would not hesitate to tackle a similar project. Knowledge – and access to the correct tools – make all the difference. With a few contractors working simultaneously, the actual work took no more than a matter of weeks. However, we would definitely approach the labour and project management aspects somewhat differently...

But getting back on the road reignited my mojo.

I felt elated.

To paraphrase Jack Kerouac, there is nowhere to go but everywhere, so we will just keep rolling under the stars.

Chapter 22

The Grand Design Finale

With our Grand Design complete(ish), it seems only right to ask virtual Kevin McCloud, who was with us every step of the way, to take you on the ultimate tour.

The Beast, Jackie and Mark's self-converted overland truck, showcases their unwavering resolve and resourcefulness. It is a true Grand Design that has overcome the challenges of material sourcing and labour set-backs. The interior is a celebration of their adventurous spirit, boasting a vibrant 'underwater' theme with scorched and stained spruce ply in mesmerising tones of turquoise and coral.

Wholeheartedly embracing their love for windsurfing and skiing, they ingeniously repurposed an old surfboard and a pair of skis as both decorative and functional elements. The ski bindings serve as towel hooks for their onboard shower and wet room, adding a playful touch to the décor.

In the heart of Jackie and Mark's overland haven lies the kitchen, where utility converges with artistic innovation. Their worktop is a showstopper – a single piece of oiled sequoia whose organic shape bewitches with its natural allure. What makes it truly remarkable is the transformation of adversity into a tactile and captivating feature.

Originally plagued with rot, the channels and curves carved out to eliminate the problem have become a work of art. Rather than conceal the evidence, Jackie and Mark embraced the sinuous lines and contours to convert what was once a challenge into a defining element of their kitchen. This one piece of wood exemplifies their exceptional skill in turning setbacks into stunning design and stands as a symbol of their perseverance and creativity. It weaves a narrative of overcoming obstacles to create opportunities into the very fabric of this extraordinary creation.

Though now they'd opt for lithium batteries, back when they started the build, concerns about ruggedness and resilience guided their choice. Still, their onboard power, water, and gas systems enable them to be self-sufficient for up to a month at a time.

As we delve deeper into this exploration masterpiece, the interior unfolds like a carefully curated tapestry of stories and surprises. The sofa, with its daring colours, adds a touch of Italian flair to this nomadic haven. Crafted in a bold camouflage pattern not only reflects their eclectic taste but also serves as a testament to their ability to instil vibrant energy into every corner. Completed only hours before they embarked on their inaugural expedition, it's almost infused with the adrenaline rush of departure day.

In the world of Grand Designs, where each detail is a chapter in the journey, this emerges as a vivid paragraph, embodying spontaneity, creativity, and the thrilling crescendo of finishing touches added just as the adventure begins.

Jackie and Mark have transformed a potential logistical nightmare into a nomadic dream.

They have proven that, with determination and ingenuity, even the most challenging Grand Designs can become a reality.

Appendix 1: Insulation

1. Battens

Miles fitted wooden battens to the ribbed interior of The Beast's cargo box to take the stained wall panels. This ensured that no interior fixings were in contact with the outside of the truck, which prevents any thermal bridging.

Tek screws, which go straight through metal without pre-drilling, were used to affix the vertical wall battens.

The profile of the metal ribs on the roof made it impossible to drill in a mechanical fixing, so the roof battens were fixed with Sikaflex bonding adhesive.

2. Insulation

Since The Beast would be our home year-round in some challenging climates, we needed her to be fit to face the extremes of both summer and winter.

We used Recticel Eurothane® GP 40mm PIR (Polyisocyanurate Rigid) insulation boards. It came highly recommended because;

- Its thermal conductivity $\lambda = 0.022$ W/mK (Watts-Per-Metre-Square-Kelvin) This is a measure of how much heat passes through each square metre of material per hour. The lower the value, the better the insulator, so a thinner layer achieves the same insulation efficiency.

- PIR has a high fire-safety value.

- The boards have a vapour barrier on both sides.

- PIR is lightweight and easy to cut.

- Recticel has similar properties to other brands, such as Celotex and Kingspan, but is generally less expensive.

40 mm was a perfect thickness to provide the insulation required. It also fitted 5 mm shy of the battens in The Beast, so it wouldn't protrude and affect fitting wall panels.

Miles placed insulation strips both behind and on top of all the truck's aluminium ribs. "It is time consuming, but it's done only once, and ensures there are no cold spots." Miles also noted – "Average sunny day in the UK. Dark roof. Roof ribs are so hot that they can't be touched for more than a few seconds! So, three layers of foiled insulation over them."

Every join on the insulation was sealed with four-inch foil tape.

The floor was also insulated similarly to the walls and roof, to ensure we'd remain toasty in winter.

3. Panels

Miles washed the spruce ply panels with watered down paint, before sanding and varnishing. The stained wooden panels were bonded, with a few hidden screws to hold them in place.

Appendix 2:
What We Would
Do Differently

A Self-Build is never finished. However good your design, there are always modifications to be made and things you want to change. After living with The Beast for some time, here are a few of the major changes, in the order in which we made them.

1. **Battery-to-Battery Charger** – in our first Season of Solar Anxiety (a British winter), we discovered that despite having "enough solar to power a rock festival," it wasn't sufficient to keep the batteries charged in the short days of a northern winter. So, Luke of Bluefix Energy Solutions Ltd fitted two Victron Orion battery-to-battery chargers to top up our leisure batteries from The Beast's alternator and starter battery every time we drive.

2. **Battery Monitor** – it was ridiculous not to have this. The display on the solar controller did not give an accurate reading of our battery bank's state of charge. We couldn't see

whether the batteries were running down, or when they were fully charged when we had the charger switched on. I am sure we over-discharged or overcharged them several times, which would have shortened their lives. Luke fitted a battery monitor at the same time as the Orion battery-to-battery chargers.

3. **90 litre LPG Tank** – we fitted this to replace the two 20 litre Safefill refillable cylinders to give us extended off grid capability. In winter, it lasts us for two months for all heating, cooking, and hot water, without the need to refill. Note that an important consideration for a single LPG container is the limit on Eurotunnel (The Channel Tunnel). This is 47 kg, or approximately 93 litres, and when travelling, each container must be no more than 80% full.

4. **800 litre Internal Water Tank** – again, to increase our off grid sustainability, and also to guarantee our water supply in winter, when our not-very-well-insulated external water tank was at risk of freezing, we added a 800 litre potable water tank internally. This enables us to carry a maximum of 1150 litres of drinking water, which is enough for six weeks.

5. **Condensation** – this is a perennial problem in RVs during the winter. Combatting it requires a balance between heat and ventilation. In Caravan Kismet, we used silica gel kitty litter in cupboards and under the bed to desiccate the air. Electrical dehumidifiers work like a fridge or air conditioning unit. Their compressors and fans are large, heavy, and energy hungry, so most won't work from a 12-volt supply. In The Beast, the roof lights still attract condensation, as do the

double-glazed windows to a lesser extent, because neither are as well insulated as the walls. One of the best purchases we've ever made is a Karcher Window Vac, which hoovers up moisture in seconds. On the bright side, vacuuming condensation from our roof lights has effectively turned them into a zero-energy dehumidifier! On cold winter nights, we install removable foam inserts into both the roof lights and windows, which keep heat in and help prevent condensation. We have also removed some compartmentalisation in storage areas to improve the air circulation and prevent damp. We invested in a damp monitor to keep an eye on moisture levels, so we can take action to heat and/or ventilate if necessary.

6. **Separating Toilet** – we switched over from the Porta Potti to a Trobolo separating toilet following our trip to Albania, where toilet chemicals and emptying facilities are as rare as a Conservative MP with a social conscience. If you have ever cohabited with a chemical free chemi khazi in 45°C (113°F) for a few days, you will understand our rationale.

7. **Victron Electrical System** – despite much tidying up, Iain's system never performed well, and we had concerns about its safety. The epithet 'Buy Cheap Buy Twice' definitely applied to our electrical set up. Also, in the intervening period, lithium battery technology improved and prices came down. Eventually, we bit the bullet and asked Mark and Luke of Bluefix Energy Solutions Ltd to replace the entire solar control system with Victron, to power a 460 Amp Hour Roamer Lithium Iron Phosphate (LiFePO4) battery. The Victron system performs much more efficiently. Spares are available worldwide. Plus, because it is a 'smart' system, the

Bluefix guys can log into it to troubleshoot wherever we are in the world. To us, that is worth its weight in gold – and has already proved its value when our battery stopped charging when we were at 1800 m in the Alps.

8. **Diesel Heater** – at the time of the build, diesel heaters were expensive and available from only a couple of suppliers. It was always our intention to fit a diesel heater as a backup for our trip to Mongolia, particularly because LPG is not available in some countries. Since then, the quality and availability of Chinese diesel heaters improved, and prices dropped. Following a chain of disasters typical of our lives, which left us without an LPG heater in a severe cold snap, our friends, Darren and Alex, kindly fitted a diesel heater. But that, like changing the tyres, is a whole other story!

Thank You!

Thank you so much for reading *Building The Beast*. The Fab Four, Mark, and I hope you enjoyed it.

If you have a moment, we would be unbelievably grateful if you could leave a review on Amazon, Goodreads, BookBub – or anywhere else – to tell others what you thought of the book.

It can be as short as you like.

I read all the reviews, so if you learned something, felt inspired, had a giggle at our misfortunes, or anything else, a single sentence will make my day. Not only that, honest reviews help readers to find my books. As an independent author, I don't have the marketing might of a publishing company behind me, so your reviews and ratings really matter.

And if you want to be the first to know when I release a new book, here are a few ways to keep in touch:

- Facebook:

    ◦ https://www.facebook.com/JacquelineLambertAuthor

- Amazon:

    ◦ https://www.amazon.com/author/JacquelineLambert

- Goodreads:

  - https://www.goodreads.com/author/show/18672478.Jacqueline_Lambert

- Bookbub:

  - https://www.bookbub.com/profile/jacqueline-lambert

- Blog:

  - https://www.WorldWideWalkies.com

Besides stories and photos from our travels, my blog has tips and printable checklists for travel with dogs, details of how we fund our lifestyle, and links to suppliers we used in the construction of The Beast.

I am also a member of We Love Memoirs, the friendliest group on Facebook.

WLM connects readers and authors to discuss all kinds of memoirs, including travellers' 'tails' like this one.

If memoirs, competitions, or book giveaways are your thing, pop in and say 'Hi' there too!

Thank you!

By The Same Author:

Adventure Caravanning with Dogs Series

Year 1 – Fur Babies in France – From Wage Slaves to Living the Dream

The true story of a couple who accidentally bought their first caravan – then decided to give up work, rent out the house, and tour Europe full time with their four dogs. This book follows their first year on wheels, which involved lots of breakages, and a near death experience on Day 1...

"Full of fun. Told with excitement, vibrancy, and humour." Julie Haigh, Goodreads Librarian and Top 1.000 Amazon Reviewer

"Well written, full of bounce and fun." Valerie Poore, Author and blogger at Marvellous Memoirs: Reviews and links

Dog on the Rhine – From Rat Race to Road Trip

Now, with a little caravanning experience under their belts, the crew get a bit more adventurous and cross Germany, before going on a brief bark around the Balkans (the Czech Republic, Slovenia and Croatia). But lest they mislead you into thinking that Livin' the Dream is all sunshine and rainbows, they return home to a huge Fidose of reality…

"An inspirational travelogue." Windyoneuk on Amazon.co.uk

"Makes me want to take my dog, buy a caravan, and go traveling." Chris on Goodreads

Dogs 'n' Dracula – A Road Trip Through Romania

Told they would be robbed, scammed, kidnapped by gypsies, eaten by bears or attacked by wild dogs and wolves, if they managed to avoid the floods, riots – and vampires – the team Boldly Go Where No Van Has Gone Before. Join them as they explore Europe's largest wilderness, adopt a street dog, and tow a caravan across the Carpathian Mountains on one of the world's most dangerous roads.

WINNNER: Chill With A Book Premier Readers' Award, 2022

FINALIST: Romania Insider Awards for Best Promotion of Romania Abroad, 2019

"Armchair travel delight." Frances Hampson on Amazon.com
"A delightful book about the nomad lifestyle." Sharon Geitz, Gum Trees and Galaxies

It Never Rains But It Paws – A Road Trip Through Politics And A Pandemic

Five years after giving up work to travel full-time, Jackie and Mark race against time to leave the UK before Britain exits the EU. If Brexit happens, their four precious pups will lose their pet passports and will be unable to travel. But Brexit isn't their only obstacle. How do they cope when, a few months into their trip, the pandemic leaves them trapped in the epicentre of Europe's No.1 coronavirus hotspot?

"Her nimble writing rivals Bill Bryson and Paul Theroux." Liisa W. on Amazon.com

"A very light-hearted and enjoyable read." Alison Williams (author), Alison Williams Writing

To Hel in a Hound Cart – Journey To The Centre Of Europe

"Go to Hel!" The local wasn't being rude. She was describing Poland's best beach and windsurfing destination. Released from coronavirus lockdown, Jackie and Mark packed themselves and four dogs into their hound cart (RV), but are unsure where their wanderlust might take them. Their adventures soon start stacking up. Dodging precipitous cliff-side roads, political unrest, and a global pandemic, will they make it to Hel in a Hound Cart, or is that what will happen to their plans?

"Exuberant, sparkling with wit, insights, and well-researched historical facts... it's laugh-out-loud, poignant, and superbly written." Fi Kidd, Overland Adventurer

"Her irrepressible sense of irreverent humour and quest for knowledge once more shine through." Sue Bavey, Author of Lucky Jack (1894-2000)

Although part of a series which is chronological in time, and follows the author since giving up work to travel, each book is a standalone adventure.

Pups on Piste – A Ski Season in Italy

Jackie, Mark, and their canine crew spend three months in Monte Rosa, a little-known ski resort tucked under the second highest peak in Western Europe. It also happens to be in the world's Top 5 off-piste ski destinations. With parables from on piste and off, our snowmads get lost, stranded – and are told by an instructor, "Don't miss the turn or you'll go over a cliff."

"Highly recommended for dog lovers, ski enthusiasts, and adventure travellers." Louise Capper, Waggy Tales Book & Dog Blog.

"Excellent reference book! Jackie's story telling and informative approach has not only relieved me of some of my anxieties (about a planned trip) but really inspired me! Most interesting is that it's a thoroughly good read by a very eloquent writer." Hannah James – Winterised.com Motorhome Skiing

The Wayward Truck Series

Building The Beast – How (Not) To Convert An Overland Campervan chronicles Jackie and Mark's misadventures when they buy an army truck blind off the internet on Friday 13th, then attempt their first ever DIY campervan conversion. Their intention is to create a tiny home fit to undertake an overland expedition to Mongolia.

Forthcoming books will follow the adventures of The Beast, their wayward truck. Initially, because of coronavirus, their expeditions are *More Manchester Than Mongolia*. Subsequently, they set off east... But will they make it to Mongolia?

Anthologies

Travel Stories Series & Box Set, Curated by Alyson Sheldrake

Itchy Feet: Tales of travel and adventure

Come with us as we take an epic journey out of Africa, through the Indonesian jungle and raft the Zambezi. Ride a Harley through France and Spain and find out what makes someone a perpetual nomad. Itchy Feet was released to a string of five-star reviews. A free photo album accompanies each book in the Travel Stories series.

> *"An excellent choice for lovers of travel and adventure stories. It's one to dip in and out of or immerse oneself in. Either way, it's a thoroughly entertaining read." Beth Haslam, Vine Voice Reviewer and Author of the Fat Dogs and French Estates series*

Wish You Were Here: Holiday Memories

Whether it is a childhood 'bucket and spade' family holiday, the 'once-in-a-lifetime' dream destination, your first trip abroad, or the city where you first fell in love, we all have that one holiday that stands out in our minds. The award-winning and top travel memoir authors in this anthology bring out their postcards and photo albums and invite you to join them as they reminisce about their travels. Maybe they will inspire you to book your next holiday too!

> *"From Paris to Galapagos – from the comfort of our armchair – you'll wish you were there too." Jules Brown, Author of the Born to Travel Series: Tales from a Travel Writer's Life.*

The Travel Stories Box Set

With 17 (yes – *seventeen*) bonus chapters, including *A Honeymoon Horror Story* by yours truly, that's nearly a whole extra book!

Robert Fear Anthologies

40 Life Changing Events, 2022 edition

25 writers share events that have changed their lives. Some of these stories are tragic, others full of joy, but they all encapsulate tenacity, resilience, and self-belief. This fascinating compilation will encourage you to pause and reflect, with tales that offer much needed motivation and inspiration in these challenging times.

"From a letter to a past lover to the Namibian desert, dogs and thieves, there is a wealth of experiences to enjoy." Fabulouschrissie on Amazon.com

50 Intriguing Personal Insights, 2023 edition

In this anthology of real-life stories, twenty-nine writers share fifty fascinating experiences about themselves or those close to them. Take a break from your busy schedule and immerse yourself in this remarkable book. Discover how pivotal moments have affected their lives in unpredictable ways. You will feel stimulated by their honesty and take away a sense of intrigue and fulfilment.

"Another great collection. You can read it all in one – or it's perfect for dipping in and out of, a few stories at a time." Julie Haigh, Amazon Top 1,000 reviewer.

30 Evocative Recollections, 2024 edition

18 authors share the moving experiences that shaped them. From childhood memories to adult revelations, from tragedies to triumphs, these stories will touch your heart, and inspire you to reflect on your own journey.

"Tinges of longing, loss, joy, and redemption." Ronald Mackay, Author.

Follow this link to find all of Jacqueline's books on your local Amazon store: https://author.to/JLambert

Preview From My Next Book: 'More Manchester Than Mongolia'

How To Make A Four Month Trip Last Fourteen Years!

I have written this chapter in the vernacular. I hope it makes sense. If you struggle with the Yorkshire dialect, there is a short Yorkshire/English glossary at the end. The rest of the book is written in plain English!

"**M**ark. We didn't run anyone over when we parked, did we?"

We had arrived late on Saturday night at the Bridestones, an isolated spot high on the moors above Hebden Bridge in Yorkshire. At 9 a.m. on Sunday, as Mark and I descended the steps to take our pups out for their morning constitutional, we saw two pairs of legs, clad in bright orange high visibility overalls, sticking out from beneath our truck.

As we clattered down the steps, the legs spoke.

"Eyup! Ah didn't realise there were anyone in!"

A slim, grey-haired chap slid out from under the truck, followed by his stockier, black-haired mate. Both sporting full Hi Vis onesies.

"We were lookin' at yer axles! Ah heard voices and thought Ah better introduce meself!" the older gentleman addressed me. "Tek this down, lass. You know how to do Google and that, don't ya? Look me up; 'Ian Coates Honda'. Ah can do work on this truck. This is me apprentice, Willie. 'E's in 'is fifties now though. Ah'm seventy five!"

That was our introduction to Yorkshire's equivalent of Fred Dibnah, Lancashire's highly colourful and much-loved old school steeplejack-cum-steam-traction-engine guru who had his own television series, simply called 'Fred'.

We invited Ian and Willie in for a brew (a cup of tea), for which they reciprocated with truck wisdom and entertainment. Ian shared his life story,

"Ah'll tell ya this. A bloke asked me to go to get 'is motorbike from Johannesburg. Ah said, 'wheer's Johannesburg? Is it in Wales?' 'E said, 'No, it's in Africa!' So, Ah said, 'Wheer's it near?' 'E said, 'Cape Town.'

"Well, Ah said to me missus, 'Ah'll be gone four month,' so Ah set off and got tuh Africa. Ah went along a bit, then a country wouldn't let me in. Ah stopped at a shop wi' a phone and rang t'bloke wi' t'motorbike. 'What country you in?' he asked. Ah asked lass in t'shop.

'Kenya,' she said. 'What town,' 'e asked. 'Nairobi' It were Sudan wouldn't let me in.

"Well, Ah thought, there's me motorbike in t'cowshed, so Ah phoned our lad and said, 'Pack that up and send it tuh Nairobi.' Then Ah phoned our lass an' said, 'Ah'm gonna be gone longer than four month!'

"Ah went round Africa for four year on me bike! Ah went to Johannesburg, then Malawi an' Namibia. Ah nipped into Sudan – under t'radar, like. Then Ah asked, 'Wheer's Egypt?' Ah didn't 'ave a map. Yuh don't need a map.

"Then, Ah asked, 'Wheer's Argentina?' So, Ah had me bike shipped out there! There were snow on t'ground. Silly buggers there 'ave winter in July! Ah asked, 'Wheer's Alaska? Ah'm gonna go there!' So, Ah rode me bike all t'way up America. Ah were gone fourteen year!"

"You were gone for fourteen years!" Mark and I exclaimed. "What on earth did your wife think?"

"Judith? Eeeh, when Ah got back, she 'ad a face like a bulldog suckin' p*** off a thistle!"

Ian shared some tips on safety while travelling. Pointing at me, he said,

"When someone comes knockin' by surprise, you need to say, 'Oh. Ah thought it were Frank. I'm expecting Frank and 'is son.' Then they'll think you've got someone comin' and you'll be safe."

After tea, we all went back outside. Willie had a look under the hood and showed Mark how to use the tyre inflator that runs off the brake compressor. He also told us we need to grease our nipples weekly. Mark and I caught each other's gaze. We didn't know we had nipples to grease, but we do love a double entendre.

The next surreal moment of the day was when Ian and Willie took Mark off to see their workshop. I found myself sitting in the truck with the dogs all alone, with no phone, because that was in Mark's pocket. I locked the door and spent the next ninety minutes wondering whether they had actually kidnapped my husband. If they had, I was well and truly stuck. Due to coronavirus lockdowns, I'd been unable to have truck driving lessons.

You get a feeling about people, and I reckoned Ian and Willie were good eggs, although I noted the registration number of Ian's Land Rover. Just in case.

In due course, Mark returned with Ian and his wife Judith, a grease gun ("a solid one you can ram right in"), and a couple of tubes of grease.

Ian stared at me with eyes like lasers. "Who are you expectin'?" he asked.

"Frank!" I replied.

"And?" Ian didn't drop his gaze.

"Frank and 'is son!"

"Good lass!" Ian beamed.

They both came in for a cuppa. Judith was a sweetheart. A tiny slender lady with a serene face, framed by wispy grey hair, swept back into a ponytail. Her gentle demeanour belied a core of quiet Yorkshire grit. I asked her,

"How did you get on with him gone for fourteen years?!"

"Oh. It were alright!" she sighed. "Ah 'ad me kids and grandkids. An' Ah used to fly out and meet 'im every now and again."

I got the impression she had quite enjoyed the peace.

Clearly, the meeting at Ian's place had gone swimmingly. "You should see his yard," Mark told me. "It's amazing!"

Then Mark laughed as he prompted Ian,

"Tell Jackie why they threw you out of Kazakhstan."

With a massive grin and twinkling eyes, Ian told the tale.

"Well, Ah got to't border and Ah were all set. They stamped me passport and everythin', then they asked what Ah was wantin' to do there, so Ah told 'em. 'Ah've come to see wheer Borat lived.'

"And they chucked me out!

"Ah spoke to me mate and told 'im, 'They chucked me out o'Kazakhstan!' and 'e said,

"'Yer didn't mention Borat did yer?'

"So Ah said, 'Ah did!' and 'e said, 'Yer daft 'apeth!'"

In case you're not familiar, *Borat* is a controversial mockumentary comedy film whose lead character, Borat Sagdiyev, is an anti-Semitic Kazakh journalist, played by actor Sacha Baron Cohen. Personally, I love Baron Cohen's trademark of shockingly exaggerated characters who poke fun at racism and prejudice. However, it does not make him popular in all circles. Particularly those who take British satire and self-deprecating humour literally.

Kazakhstan and Russia banned the film *Borat*. According to the news agency Pravda, the film left the Kazakhs feeling furious and humiliated, and Baron Cohen received death threats.

Ian's travels had taken him to almost every country in the world. He told us all kinds of stories. At one point, he told us he was teaching English in a girls' school.

"Ah taught 'em to sing '*On Ilkley Moor Bah t'At*'. That took about two week. After that, Ah taught 'em '*The Lassie from Lancashire*' – then Ah thought, 'Oh no! Ah've taught 'em to sing it in a Yorkshire accent! But Ah don't reckon anyone would know."

There is a fierce rivalry between the northern English counties of Lancashire and Yorkshire. It goes back all the way to the Wars of the Roses between 1455 and 1487, when the houses of York and Lancaster battled it

*out for the British throne. It ended when Henry Tudor
slaughtered the last king standing, Richard III, at the
Battle of Bosworth Field.*

*The Lancashire/Yorkshire rivalry applies in all in-
stances, unless Lankies and Yorkies come together 'Down
South', in which case, we all identify as 'Northerners'
and present a united front in opposition to the Southern
Shandy-drinking Softies!*

In addition to a grease gun, Mark came back with a list of maintenance tasks. In my innocence, I had believed that the truck was similar
to a car, and only required an annual service.

"Tek this down, lass," Ian instructed. "You need to mek a list of
spares and maintenance things and tick it off when it's done to keep
track. If you don't keep yer nipples greased, yer prop shaft can seize. If
owt else goes wrong, you can still drive. But if yer prop shaft goes, yer
well and truly stuck..."

Mark revelled in his newfound knowledge regarding which of the
six were the drive wheels. Like the rest of her, The Beast's tyres looked
brand new. Although 30-years old, they had done fewer than 6000
km (4000 miles). Ian explained the new regulations for coaches and
lorries, which would require the tyres on the steering wheels to be
fewer than ten years old. That was thrilling news; we had thought the
regs applied to all tyres, so it meant we only needed to change the two
front tyres, rather than the full half dozen. As yet, we had no inkling
of the tyre-related Pandora's Box that lay in wait. Ian hinted at it as he
pressed home the benefit of us carrying both spare wheels.

"You have split rim wheels. They call them 'widow makers'. They have to be inflated in a cage. If you get a puncture, no-one will want to change one of those at t'roadside."

So, besides greasing our nipples weekly – or possibly monthly with our mileage – we needed to stock up on Type 30 brake diaphragms, bleed the brake air tanks daily – or weekly with our mileage – to get rid of water condensed in the tanks, and change our front tyres in the next few months, before the new legislation came in.

Mark and I gave ourselves a virtual high five. We had a maintenance schedule and knew our drive wheels from our steering wheels. I even managed to score a maintenance manual for the Volvo N10 from the internet. We were really getting the hang of this truckin' mullarkey.

Or so we thought.

Yorkshire/English Translation

- **Tenses** – In Yorkshire dialect, verb tenses and participles are mixed around, e.g. **Ah were doin' summat** instead of 'I was doing something', or **I was stood** instead of I was standing.

- **Dropped Letters**

  ○ Letters are often dropped from the beginning and end of words, such as **'E** (He) and **Goin'** (Going).

  ○ Aitches are always dropped.

  ○ Plurals – the S is frequently dropped, so 'four months' becomes 'four month'.

- **Pronunciation** – think professional Yorkshireman, Actor Sean Bean!

Glossary

- **Ah** – I

- **Apeth** – Literally a Halfpenneth or Halfpennyworth, but used as an affectionate term for a silly person, as in 'you daft apeth'.

- **Aht** – Out or outside

- **Bloke** – Man

- **Brew** – Cup of Tea

- **Eyup!** – 'Hello', or an exclamation along the lines of Flipping Heck!

- **Lass** – Girl *(see also **Ahr lass** below)*

- **Me** – My

- **Mek** – Make

- **Meself** – Myself

- **Missus** – Wife

- **On Ilkley Moor Baht 'At** – On Ilkley Moor without a hat; Yorkshire's unofficial anthem

- **Ahr lad** – 'Our lad' – means my son

- **Ahr lass** – 'Our girl' – my wife

- **Owt** – Anything (Nowt is nothing)

- **T'** – The. Sometimes the definite article is also dropped completely, as in – 'I asked lass in t'shop'

- **Tek** – Take

- **Tuh** – To

- **Wheer** – Where

- **Ya** – You

- **Yer** – You or Your

About The Author

J acqueline (Jackie) Lambert is an award-winning travel writer, adventure traveller, and dogmother, who loves history and curious
facts.

BC (Before Canines) she rafted, rock-climbed, and backpacked
around six of the seven continents. A passionate windsurfer and skier,
she can fly a plane, has been bitten by a lion, and appeared on Japanese
TV as a fire-eater.

AD (After Dog), she quit work in 2016 to hit the road permanently
with her husband and four pooches. Initially, they were Adventure
Caravanners, who aimed To Boldly Go Where No Van Has Gone
Before.

Now, they're at large in a self-converted six-wheel army lorry, with
Mongolia in their sights.

*All her books and the anthologies that include her travel stories are
available on Amazon: https://author.to/JLambert*

Mark, Jackie & The Fab Four with The Beast. Photo courtesy of @Liveration, who made a short film about The Beast on YouTube.

Acknowledgements

I would like to thank the following people:

100 Covers – for the wonderful book cover design.

Caroline Smith – for friendship, company, and eagle-eyed editing.

The 'B' Team – (Really an 'A' Team of Wonderful Beta Readers) **Judith Benson, Jan Butterfield, Catherine Cummins, Chris Evans, Julie Haigh, Rebecca Hislop, Kari Iverson Lane, Susan Jackson, Stephen Malins, Veronica Moore, Valerie Poore, Anna Rashbrook, Sue Raymond, Carrie Riseley, Alyson Sheldrake, and Lisa Rose Wright**

for kindly reading my manuscript and offering their valuable feedback.

To Mark, Cody, and the team at the Hoghton Arms in Withnell, Lancashire, who hosted us in our hour of need, and which is where much of this book was written.

My Readers Around the World – as authors, we bare our souls for your entertainment. Your kind words, reviews, and encouragement mean so much.

And of course, Mark, Kai, Rosie, Ruby and Lani for filling my everyday with unconditional love.

Dog Bless You All!

I can't end without a special tribute to Oscar the Spinone, The Fab Four's special friend and Caroline and
Graham's gentle giant. In February 2024, he crossed
the rainbow bridge in the Ayas Valley, in sight of
Monte Rosa. It's where he was most happy and where
he belonged. Now, he will never have to leave.

Oscar

2010 – 2024

RIP